MW01632287

15 DAYS

DR. COREY THOMPSON

TABLE OF CONTENTS

My baby is coming home today!"
-April, 28, 2010, Milwaukee's Mitchell International Airport, Milwaukee, Wisconsin
(Words spoken by a very excited American mom as she is about to be re-united with her nine year old daughter who has recently completed a 15 day international fieldtrip to Denmark.)

"Travel is a vital component
of the educational experience for Americans of all ages."
-Congress of the United States of America (2003)

"That dude is awesome!"
-Urban Ecology Center, Milwaukee, Wisconsin
staff member, speaking about MPS veteran teacher Mark Horowitz
(summer, 2010)

"Denmark is a means to an end..."
-Mr. Dick Marx, 2-time Chaperone
(April 27, 2011, Mitchell International Airport,
minutes from departure of the 17th trip)

In Memory of Mr. Kamonie Slade, our friend
June 14, 2010
An MPS Student who left us way too soon!

ACKNOWLEDGEMENTS

This work could not have been possible were it not for the collective efforts of several individuals. First and foremost, as cliché as it may sound, I would like to thank God for the opportunity to be in the position to write this text. I strongly believe each of us was put on this earth to perform a task or tasks; to use our God-given gifts to complete these tasks. Some people spend their entire lifetime trying to determine what it is they are to do during their time on earth. I am most thankful that I discovered early on in life that I wanted to be an educator. And since that revelation, I have spent every day of my life educating and empowering students and teachers.

I know that my love for education comes first and foremost from my very first teachers-my parents Herman and Eddneata Thompson. Despite being young parents and still enrolled in college, they made a decision to not only stay together and get married, but to finish their degrees, while being humble enough to provide shelter for the three of us in a Howard Johnson's motel(I have often pondered writing a memoir of my life titled From Ivory Soap to the Ivory Towers, chronicling my life's journey from a poor African-American boy living in a motel to my career as a private university professor... but that is for a later date!).

Fast forward a few years, I will never forget the day I came home from college to find our basement filled with personal items not belonging to us. When I was told that the items belonged to one of my mom's students, I was amazed to find out that my mom was slowly, but surely, helping this student leave her abusive husband. I was amazed that this English teacher, whose job it was to teach English, was actually empowering her student to make a better future for herself. From that moment on, I knew I wanted to be a teacher! Mom, this book, this story of the power of an individual teacher, is for you!

I would also like to acknowledge the many fine educators I have been blessed to have had as my teachers throughout my K-12 experience. One always runs the risk of leaving someone out when individually recognizing people by name; however, I am going to take the risk that if the reader had been one of my teachers and does not find his or her name mentioned that he or she will not be offended. In no particular order or preference, I am the educator I am today because of the likes of Mr. Brugger, Mr. Jerry Burgher, Mrs. Blanche Troutman, Mrs. Mary Satterwaite, Mr. Tom Herbek and a whole cast of teachers who comprised the faculty of Rufus King Middle School. Middle school can be a challenging time in the life of an adolescent. I have nothing but the fondest of memories of my middle school experience and I know it is due to the learning environment you all collectively helped to establish. I am confident I became a middle school teacher because of your collective influence!

To Mr. Glassnapp, Mr. Ptak, Mr. Bland and the many fine teachers at "Prephouse!". To this day, I remain convinced that I am the person I am today because of the four wonderful years I spent at Rufus King High School for the College Bound in Milwaukee, Wisconsin.

Soccer is life! End of story, or EOS as "fella" would say. To that end, I would like to acknowledge the many coaches and teammates and opponents I have had the pleasure of working with on the soccer field-my other classroom! I am eternally grateful for having been a part of a team sport like soccer. I have learned so many life lessons from the "beautiful game". As the young people would say, I would like to give a special "shout out" to "fella" (mentioned above). You know who you are and I am proud to call you my former co-captain, teammate, opponent going back to our days of Sherman Park versus Mid City, current teammate reuniting the "U" and now fellow educator!

I would also like to give a special thank you to Mr. Tim Mattner, one of my former graduate students. Tim was a student in our Kenosha MAT (Master's of Art in Teaching) cohort. One day in class, Tim planted the idea in my mind for writing a book. Tim's original idea was for me to shadow MAT students and provide support and assistance in the form of classroom management-in somewhat similar fashion to the very popular TV show The Nanny, in which the nanny shows parents how to effectively raise their children. I was intrigued by the possibility of working alongside my former students in their classrooms but, I do thank you Tim for your confidence in me to be of service to new teachers in their journey to become effective classroom managers. It is my hope and desire that this book will accomplish the same goal by allowing new teachers to dream big in their classrooms, to learn to love their craft, to commit to becoming life-time learners and to truly understand what it takes and what it means to make learning come alive for children.

I would also like to acknowledge the collective influence of my extended family, including the family I married into. Collectively, you have supported our family in so many ways that I do not have the words to say how much you mean to me! Whether it is your overwhelming kindness during the holidays or your general love and support of the many efforts my children are involved in throughout the year, I am eternally grateful. Blood is thicker than water.

This book is about an amazing teacher and the incredible children he has had the pleasure of teaching over the years, but the book is also about the many, many Danish families who say "Yes!" to this incredible responsibility, year after year. And so, to the Herskind family and Charlotte and Torben: there are not enough words to express how genuinely grateful we are that you have opened your homes to our children and me. We often tell people we have family "overseas", and it is true!

Finally, to my immediate family: my wife Kiki and our beautiful children-Abby, Benjamin, Maggie and Katherine. I would be remiss to not mention the foster children we have had the privilege of raising over the years: Abigail, Joseph, Noel, Briana, and our God-children: Angelo, Will and Rachel! You are my "raison d'etre"! This work could not have been produced without your love, support and inspiration.

TAK. TUSINTAK. MANGETAK.

In Memory of

MR. KAMONIE SLADE, OUR FRIEND

June 14, 2010

An MPS Student who left us way too soon!

FOREWORD

BY EDDNEATA THOMPSON

Since the early 1970s, I have guided three generations of sons-three sons ten and twelve years apart-through the Milwaukee Public School system. It has required constant navigation, with eyes and ears on constant lookout for word of a good school. I compare it to the experiences of one-celled animals in a drop of pond water observed through a microscope. There is constant movement as the protozoa bang against other cell walls, react and float away into the next obstacle.

Because I was trained as a teacher, I was aware of what was going on in the public schools from my own experiences, conversations with other teachers and teacher relatives. It was obvious most parents kept eyes and ears open for news of a good school. Parents, who could afford to, moved to the suburbs or as in my case, reacted by sending their children to private schools, typically Catholic schools known for strict discipline and good standardized test scores.

In the late 70s, my oldest son, Corey, was in third grade at a small Catholic school where a friend's current husband had recently been a priest. This was a K-8 school and we were satisfied with our son's progress, but it happened that a new plan was being proposed by the current superintendent of Milwaukee Public Schools. The idea was to develop "specialty schools" within the system to attract city wide interest in the city's school system. Fourth Street School, with grades three through five, would be the school for the "gifted and talented". And what parent doesn't think her child isn't gifted and talented? My son had started reading at age four. When he was four months old, his uncle swore that he had said "area is equal to pi r squared". I never heard those sounds, but I kept listening to verify that he had indeed said them.

After much media discussion of the specialty schools, I took a day off work to visit Fourth Street School. I did not want to announce my visit; I wanted to see the real thing.

When I arrived at the school and managed to find the office, immediately I met a group of charming and smiling office personnel. I had been in enough schools to know that this group would decide if I got a chance to talk to the principal.

When I was finally ushered into the principal's office, I met the most charismatic personality-Mr. Albin Kaczmarek. Mr. Kaczmarek was proud of his school. As he walked with me through the hallways and pointed out classrooms, we passed by students he called by names and asked about people and events in their lives. Over the years I observed that this man made the school. He expected much from his teachers and students and they delivered. He told the students they were special and important and they believed him.

In 2009, I was at the fifth grade graduation at Golda Meir School and the current principal has that same "Kaczmarek" attitude. The students at this school continue to perform. It continues to be a clean attractive school, decorated with student art and projects.

I made an appointment to bring my son back for a visit and at the end of that visit I filled out an application. I wasn't even aware that there could be a choice of a teacher. The problem would be being accepted. It would be done by a computer and at that time there was a requirement to keep the school racially balanced.

My reaction to obstacle number one was to come home and call my son's uncle who was a principal in the system and ask him to talk to someone at central office.

When school began in the fall, we were happy for several reasons. There was great expectation for the new specialty schools; we were happy that our child was enrolled in fourth grade at the school for the gifted and talented, a good school which would not require tuition payments. The previous spring, we had purchased our first home and we would be reaping the benefits of our property tax dollars. We had met the teacher, Mark Horowitz, a balding genie with eyes that twinkled when he spoke of his students. I had volunteered to come into the classroom two days a week to listen to children read. So Corey's mother and baby brother in the carrier became a familiar sight at Fourth Street School.

The first year I volunteered to be in charge of the communication committee; the committee in charge of the confetti of flyers that went home with the students on a regular basis.

I do not remember my first impression of Mark Horowitz, but my most memorable impression of him occurred early in October at the first open house. Three flyers preceded the event; therefore, the event was definitely the center of conversation at our house. Open house is generally an event of "Hello, how are you?" It is not intended to be a conference where questions and discussions happen, but my husband always has an onslaught of questions and on the night of open house, Corey Thompson's parents showed up with a thick legal pad with a lot of questions.

When we finally edged our way into the crowded room, Mark Horowitz was polite, sat with us, and began to answer questions. As the line grew, I think he realized he could be in that room and with that set of parents all night. Finally he said very kindly, "Look, leave his education to me. That is my job." I don't remember if the slow anger I began to feel came across in my tone. "No, I am sorry," I said. "He is our son and his education is our responsibility. You have a classroom full of children, but this one is our responsibility". Mr. Horowitz earned my profound respect when he replied, "You know, you are right and I am sorry". I do not remember what else he said, but the fact that we were on the same page about my child's education won me over as his number two fan. Corey is his number one fan!

Watching Mr. Horowitz teach, I see that he is a spasm of energy and intellect. He engages students through his own intense interest in learning. I was not surprised when twenty-eight years later Corey and his wife decided to take their oldest daughter out of their church school at the end of second grade and enroll her at Golda Meir. Mark Horowitz became her fourth grade teacher. He is currently my grandson's teacher and I suspect that he will be around to teach my two other granddaughters as well!

When I visit programs at Golda Meir, I am still impressed with the environment of success that weaves itself throughout the school. When we attend grandparent luncheons or student award days, I climb the steps to say hello to Mark Horowitz. New teachers are here, but his energy is still very much evident.

When one hears about a wonderful teacher in a really great school, one really wants to spread the word. Over the years, I have told a lot of parents about the wonderful Golda Meir experience.

CHAPTER 1

THE MAN

The fall of 1978 brought about many firsts for me. It would be my first year attending public schools. I was to begin fourth grade at Fourth Street School in Milwaukee, Wisconsin after having spent kindergarten through third grade at Catholic schools in the city of Milwaukee. I do not know what caused my parents to make the change from Catholic schools to public schools, but I am eternally grateful that they did and you will understand why later on in this journey. I have nothing against Catholic schools; in fact I work very closely with many of them today as an educational consultant, not to mention that my full time employment is supported by a Catholic institution of higher learning; however, nothing compares to having "the man" as one's teacher.

The 1978-1979 school year would also "mark" (no pun intended!) the first time that neither my mom nor my dad would drive me to and from school. I would now start taking a big yellow school bus to and from school from our house wonderfully nestled in the Sherman Park neighborhood on Milwaukee's Westside. I had loved being driven to and from school every day by my parents; however, the new found independence that the bus provided opened up new doors and experiences-a phenomenon that would come back and hit me head on as I got to know "the man".

The "first" that was probably the most significant for me in 1978(although I was not cognizant of this fact at the time) was that up until that school year, all of my teachers had been European(or white, or Caucasian or whatever term one prefers) and female, some of whom were nuns wearing the traditional habit. I had no problems with having white female teachers. I had loved school, loved my teachers and I am eternally grateful for the many, many excellent white females I have had as teachers. You are grossly underpaid while serving in a career that is at the cornerstone of our world's survival!

But in 1978, I was placed in Mr. Mark Horowitz's class. He would be my very first male classroom teacher. He would also be my first Jewish teacher. Soon enough, he would become (and to this day remains) my favorite teacher. Whether my parents requested a male teacher or whether I was randomly placed in his class, I do not know. One thing I do know is I and the other twenty plus fourth graders chosen to be in his room would never be the same after a year with him. Former Golda Meir student and classmate of mine Heather Felton said of Mr. Horowitz "OMG, OMG.....he was the best thing that ever happened to me...no seriously!" I know the feeling Heather!

I know some people have a tendency to block out certain years of school as being ones they would like to forget. I do not have that problem at all! If anything, it is quite the exact opposite. My recollection of my time in Mr. Horowitz's class is very vivid:

- I remember his sense of humor. Only "mature" fourth graders would really be able to relate to him!
- I remember the field trip to Mr. Perkin's soul food restau-

rant and being interviewed by local news reporters about the experience.

- I remember my first experience camping and playing flashlight tag, making dinner with my "unicorn" group and row boating for the first time ever…not to mention starting a fire without matches!
- I remember the many, many opportunities to do hands on learning projects! It is amazing how many ideas in education seem to be recycled as I am quite sure 1978 was way before the label of "hands on learning" became a popular educational buzzword.
- I remember all of the walking field trips to downtown Milwaukee and the now defunct Triple E field trip program that allowed students to plan their own experiential learning opportunities to places around the city. To me, this was very exciting! To this day, I have seen very few educational initiatives that resemble anything like Triple E. Mr. Horowitz still teases me about my Triple E trip to the local breweries!

1978 would also "mark" the first time I had ever gone camping in my life. Camping in my immediate family consisted of trips to the Holiday Inn at best! But in the family known as Room 23, outdoor camping was a part of how we learned. Some thirty years after that experience, camping remains a steady, integral part of Mr. Horowitz's curriculum. It may come as no surprise to the reader that it is also a favorite within my own family.

Let me introduce "the man" to the reader. Mark Horowitz was born April 17, 1946 in New York, New York to Stanley and Ann Horowitz. Mark's sister Miriam provides a glimpse into the Horowitz family: "Our parents were intelligent, idealistic and tremendously hard-working. Somehow they instilled that work ethic in us. It is a family tradition to throw ourselves into our work. The way we do things can simply be described as thoroughly driven (sic)! My younger sister Susan was a chaperone on the Denmark trip in 2009 and she is going again in 2011. She directs an outreach program at the University of Hawaii that brings the latest in film and video to photographers and artists in Honolulu. She works 16 hours a day at her job, as do I in my laboratory at the University of Michigan. As does Mark, who has worked until 1:00 a.m. for most of his teaching career, preparing materials for his fourth graders." I can attest to Miriam's statements as I have been on the receiving end of a 1 a.m. Mark Horowitz email!

Miriam says it is no accident to his success in the classroom. It is the product of long hours, insight into children's interests and emotions and tremendous motivation to make them happy. His sister also attributes Mark's success as a teacher to their Aunt Henriette Janke's influence. "Our aunt was a teacher in our elementary school. She was a genius in the classroom and Mark had her as a teacher for one year. She brought folk music into her classroom and since she was a pianist in her off time, at times she played the piano for her students." If one were to enter Mr. Horowitz's room today, it would be common place for him to be playing the piano for his students too.

Miriam continues: "Mark and I were very close when we were growing up. One word to describe him as a child is sensitive. Actually, we were all sensitive children and I do not think he has forgotten how it feels to be a child. He was particularly aware of other people's unhappiness, and I think that is one reason he is such a nurturing teacher. He really wants the best for his students and for all children and other vulnerable people."

"Another trait that has persisted in Mark since his early childhood is his sense of humor. He could always make me laugh, and that continues to the present day. I recently found a 'family news report' that he wrote around 1957, when he was eleven years old. It is a hilarious account of family activities for one week, poking fun at all of us in his sly and mischievous way. To the present day, Mark writes up an omelet menu for our Thanksgiving reunions with a special item for each person in the family, related to their foibles and proclivities."

WHAT TIME IS DINNER?

Mark's younger sister Susan described her brother as being "intense" and "excelling at everything he did. I would always ask him for help on my school papers and I really liked how he took on all types of challenges. I am not surprised that he is a teacher who puts so much effort into his work. It's the way he likes to work! Education was so important to our father; he was always trying to teach us things and so I am not surprised to see my brother doing the types of things that he does for his students. He always wanted to make an impact in the community and I believe that is exactly what he is doing with life."

"Ethics and morality have always been very important to Mark, and he has always been intolerant of hypocrisy," says Miriam. "He believes in honesty and I think that is another character trait that finds its way into his classrooms. Mark will not avoid the hard issues, but will find a way to deal with them honestly and forthrightly." Certainly a teacher who exemplifies these characteristics could make a career for him or herself in a city like Milwaukee, Wisconsin, where our educational needs are many!

Mark Horowitz moved to Milwaukee, Wisconsin in 1966. Prior to coming to Fourth Street School, Mr. Horowitz began his teaching at Keefe Avenue School in 1969. While at Keefe Avenue, Mr. Horowitz worked with four other teachers and was able to work with a program that resembled a school within a school framework. For the last few years of his time at Keefe Avenue School, they were able to establish a cross-grade program, in which the children were with a certain group of teachers for three years, for 4th, 5th and 6th grades. Most of them did not stay with the same homeroom teacher for the three years, but they worked with all of the teachers. This group of teachers was able to create a program that allowed for students to travel outside of Keefe Avenue School on a regular basis. The program was called Triple E: Expansion of Educational Experiences Program. “I really liked the program we were able to establish at Keefe Avenue School,” says Mr. Horowitz. “Although it was not the philosophy of the entire school, we had the flexibility to plan various activities and experiences for our students…taking them all over Milwaukee to enhance their learning.” Sometimes the trips would be whole class; sometimes they would be done in small groups.

Not only was 1978 a year of firsts for this author, but for Mark Horowitz as well. The 1978-1979 school year was also his first year teaching at Fourth Street School, an urban school for gifted and talented students. In his first year at Fourth Street School, this veteran teacher brought plenty of youthful experience and strategies with him. Whereas some teachers may feel their way through a new teaching assignment, this wily veteran jumped right in, thereby providing us with quality educational opportunities from day one.

CHAPTER

THE MISSION

Teachers are the epitome of the phrase "life long learner." Upon completion of their certification program, many teachers continue with their schooling to receive a Master's degree in Education or another related field or perhaps even another related certification such as reading specialist or special education teacher; perhaps even obtaining administrative credentials. This is a good thing and serves as a great model for our students to see the value of an education.

In 1966, Mark Horowitz received a Bachelor's of Art in Psychology from the University of Rochester and then became a VISTA (Volunteer in Service to America) volunteer. In the fall of 1968 he entered the intern teaching program at the University of Wisconsin at Milwaukee and by January of 1969 started teaching at Keefe Avenue School. "Life long learning" for Mark continued with a Master's degree from the University of Wisconsin at Milwaukee in 1972. The mission would soon begin to take form.

For the ten years he was at Keefe Avenue School, Mr. Horowitz taught about the different ethnic backgrounds of the people of Milwaukee. He continued that work when he moved to Fourth Street School. In 1991, Fourth Street School (which had its name changed to "Golda Meir" during the 1979-1980 school year), began hosting 5th grade students from France. They did so for three years. That is when Mr. Horowitz decided to combine two things: studying the ethnic backgrounds of the people of Milwaukee and traveling to another country to learn about their culture.

WHY DENMARK?

One of my favorite courses to teach at my university is Education 315: Elementary/Middle School Social Studies Methods because I "teach" pre-service teachers how to teach social studies. Actually, what I do is to help them live social studies so they will be able to live social studies with their future students. As a part of living social studies, I take them to visit Mr. Horowitz's 4th grade classroom, the same exact room where I sat as a 4th grader in 1978; Room 23; Up the blue staircase in the historic Golda Meir School building. Typically I do not tell them why we are going there, except that it is a requirement of the course. What unfolds from that trip is the making of a mission unheard of in elementary schools across this nation, and perhaps our entire world. My students soon learn that these thirty some 4th graders are about to embark on the trip of a lifetime. Mark's sister Miriam Meisler worked with colleagues in Arhus, Denmark in 1976. She was the one who told him a lot about the country of Denmark. Miriam's work is in the field of genetic diseases and during a four month span from June, 1976 through September, 1976, her family lived in Arhus where she worked at the university. "We fell in love with Arhus," says Miriam. "I felt it was the place I should have been born! Of course I shared this enthusiasm with Mark, and later he was able to visit us and we had a magical visit there together." Life learning 101 about to launch!

I am quite sure at the time of those initial thoughts Mark did not realize the magnitude of his thinking. My hunch is many of the great things that happen in this world are either serendipitous or the result of great synergy among individuals. What Mr. Horowitz was about to engage in could best be described as "Imaginaction", a term I learned about from one of Mr. Horowitz's former student teachers, Mr. Pete Wilson. Mr. Wilson told me: "I tell my students that it is important to imagine their future or whatever goal they want to achieve...but then it isn't enough to stop there; we need to then put our plans into action to make what we imagine a reality." Thus the origin of the term!

As mentioned above, Mr. Horowitz was teaching at Fourth Street/Golda Meir School during a time when French students came over as exchange students. He comments about the experience: "During my years of teaching, I had seen numerous groups of foreign exchange students come to our building for a few weeks or months... and, I was, quite frankly, appalled at some of the behaviors I saw displayed by these visiting students. I couldn't believe they had traveled all this way and acted so rudely. I began to think about what it must be like to take American students abroad and what I would expect from them..."

There was also the reality of the authenticity of teaching social studies that played a part in the development of a great mission. Says Mr. Horowitz, "I really disliked the way we often went about teaching social studies in our schools. There were many times we would be studying about a region or country by reading about it in our textbook or watching a movie (more likely a film strip!) and I would say to the students 'now let's imagine as if we were there or on that street...what might we do, say or feel?'"

In 1980, Mr. Horowitz spent three weeks in Denmark learning about their educational system. He also found Denmark to have a very low crime rate and found out that Denmark was considered the best country at speaking English as a second language. He maintained contact with his hosts throughout the years.....and from there birthed the idea of taking thirty some fourth graders on a two week international field trip to the country of Denmark! Although some may think that a fourth grader is too young to handle an experience like this, Mark's sister Miriam certainly isn't one of them. "My son Danny traveled to Ireland with his class when he was in the third grade so I knew Mark's program would be OK." The mission: to provide students from Milwaukee, Wisconsin with as hands-on an experience as possible in learning about another culture. And every school year since the 1994-1995 school year, that is exactly what this incredible teacher has done.

Can you imagine what it must look like to those in the travel industry to see a group of 30 elementary age students with backpacks and luggage congregating on an airline gate, much more boarding the plane? It can certainly be overwhelming, but listen to the words of two flight attendants who, during the 2004 trip, took the time to send their remarks to Golda Meir School:

MS. MARGARET HAKUM WRITES:

To whom it may concern.

> I was the purser on a flight on which fourth grade students from Golda Meir School in Milwaukee, Wisconsin were traveling. There were 26 children traveling with 6 adult chaperones. They were traveling from Milwaukee to Copenhagen, Denmark. Here are my observations about this group: This was indeed a most delightful and well mannered group to have on board. They had obviously been 'briefed' on travel etiquette. They boarded calmly and got settled in readily. I know there had been some confusion in the boarding area as to their seats. *Neither the children nor leaders showed any signs of stress* (author's note: I have to believe that this phenomenon is a

pure manifestation of Mark Horowitz's influence). The group was very well mannered during the flight. I never saw them out of their seats or being loud. My main cabin crew gave them many compliments. I WISH WHOEVER "TRAINED" THIS GROUP COULD "TRAIN" ALL OUR PASSENGERS (note to purser: that would be Mr. Mark Horowitz! Sorry, he's taken right now!). Thank you for choosing Northwest Airlines. I hope I have the pleasure to share a flight with your students again.....

Sincerely,
Margaret Hakum,
Purser NWA 113263, Flight 53(AMS/DTW)

Ms. Hakum did not have to write this glowing letter. But I am glad she did as it speaks volumes to who Mark Horowitz is as a teacher. Make no mistake about it, this group traveling in 2004 turned some heads, and even got the attention of the pilots as they were allowed to have a look into the cockpit upon disembarkation, as noted in another complimentary letter received by Golda Meir School from a Mr. Van Eijden, another flight attendant on flight 53 that day. "Ground crew informed us that 26 kids checked in. We said 'Oh my God!' Upon embarkation it appeared that all kids behaved very well. They were polite and listened very well to their teachers. Both ground staff and crew were pleasantly surprised and impressed by the good behavior of the group. And so I made a compliment to 2 of the teachers and told them that whoever wanted to take a look into the cockpit could do so. This was done in an organized way so it didn't deregulate the disembarkation process. It was a pleasure to have them on board!"

I believe this book is rare. Being a foreign exchange student is certainly no stranger to the education world, especially at the secondary school and collegiate level. And, traveling internationally is certainly no stranger to those who have money; in fact it may even be a regular part of the upper class' way of life. Upon doing research for this book on the impact of international travel on urban elementary students, I quite honestly found nothing! Individual, urban teachers simply do not take two weeks out of their school year to travel with their students internationally. It is simply unheard of. I used several different search engines and prompts to try and find literature and research that supports such endeavors. While my hits on the phrasing "Impacts of International Travel on Urban Elementary Students" came up short, what follows is a collection of articles I did find that supported the concept of student travel and studying abroad in general.

A recent survey (2011) endorsed by the Student Youth and travel Association confirmed traveling overseas at a young age supports school performance, leads to successful careers and increases the likelihood of continued travel throughout one's life. The survey revealed that more than 88 percent of respondents that traveled before the age of 18 received a college degree, with more than a quarter of respondents going on to receive an advanced degree. Respondents also were high performers in school, achieving impressive college grade point averages. More than 81 percent of respondents achieved a college grade point average of 3.0 or higher, with more than 40 percent completing college with a grade point average greater than 3.6

These achievements are not limited to educational excellence. Half of the survey respondents who traveled before the age of 18 reported a household income of more than $75K and almost a third boasted a household income of more than $100K.

Survey respondents were asked to share the lasting impact of their travel abroad experiences. Local culture immersion provided the most lasting impact according to respondents, and almost three-quarters of these respondents credit their travel experiences with positively impacting their education and career. In fact, more than 90 percent of respondents report a willingness to participate in an educational travel experience again as an adult. While it is not surprising that more than 50 percent of respondents portray their youth travel experiences as "fun", it is notable that 40 percent of respondents report their youth travel is best described as "engaging."

The survey also revealed youth travel heavily impacts travel behavior in adulthood. Survey respondents that traveled outside North America before the age of 18 continue this trend as adults. In fact, more than 43 percent of youth travelers have visited at least ten countries outside of North America, with almost 90 percent traveling to non-English speaking destinations. Travel is considered so important to these respondents that more than 70 percent report spending at least $2,000 each year on travel, with one out of four respondents spending more than $5,000 annually.

According to Palmer (2003), as school systems wrestle with financial matters, accountability and assessment, and requirements imposed by the federal and state governments, educators (as well as the public at large) must ask whether all schools are providing all of America's children with a complete education. Palmer indicates there is no doubt our young people need to be skilled in core subjects; however, they must also be prepared for the increasingly complex world they will experience after graduation-a world that demands an understanding of other people and cultures; the ability to work in a team structure; and critical thinking, oral communication, and decision-making skills. American students, says Palmer, deserve an education that will not only provide skills in math and reading, but also equip them to meet the challenges of a demanding global society. This author believes, the sooner we can begin this process with our American young people, the better!

Student travel has been around for years as young people have had the opportunity to learn and practice some of these important skills through their schools or organizations. Whether observing national landmarks or visiting other nations, travel can have numerous benefits for students:

1. Educational travel brings history to life.
2. Educational travel gives depth to civics lessons.

3. Educational travel builds the foundation that will allow our students to succeed in a global society.
4. Educational travel completes the learning experience for students involved in the performance arts.
5. Educational travel can be the spark that "turns on" an unmotivated student.

EDUCATIONAL TRAVEL BRINGS HISTORY TO LIFE

According to Palmer (2003), History is so much more than words appearing in textbooks. The American past is filled with unique individuals who had exciting stories to tell. Their clothing, food, occupations, recreational activities and personal challenges all contribute to our knowledge of the past and help make history come alive.

A skilled teacher can inspire students. But a trip to the roots of our colonial heritage-to such places as Williamsburg or Monticello-allow students of today to see first-hand what made our forefathers who they were. Mrs. Lucy Little, long time colleague to Mark Horowitz at Golda Meir School, has taken this very trip to Colonial Williamsburg with her fourth graders for years.

According to Mcgee-Anderson (2009), allowing children to experience a world they may only ever see on TV is priceless. She recalls her own travel experience to the American South: "I remember clearly the summer when my parents took us to Memphis, Tennessee for a long weekend. Education has always been important to my family and my parents were determined that my sister and I would learn during our trip. We visited the hotel where Martin Luther King Jr. had been killed. Looking through the window of the hotel and seeing it preserved made a huge impression on me. I had always known of the Civil Rights Movement. My parents remember what it was like to have to go through the back door of restaurants if they wanted to eat. Hearing the stories did not impress me as much as seeing the Martin Luther King Museum and the hotel where he died. For the first time in my young life, I began to understand that inequality and injustice was never right. I date my activism against inequality from that trip to Memphis".

EDUCATIONAL TRAVEL GIVES DEPTH TO CIVICS LESSONS

One of the frequent criticisms of young people and the American population as a whole, according to Palmer (2003), is that young people have a lack of involvement in the governing process. Schools can set the foundation for voting in national elections and participating in the democratic process. And why wouldn't they given the turnout record we have posted in the United States of America, as illustrated in Table 1 below (obtained from www.infoplease.com). Students who travel might be able to change the demographics regarding those who participate in our democratic voting process.

Table 1

NATIONAL VOTER TURNOUT IN FEDERAL ELECTIONS: 1960-2008

Year	Voting-age population	Voter registration	Voter turnout	Turnout of voting-age population (percent)
2008*	**231,229,580**	**NA**	**132,618,580***	**56.8%**
2006	220,600,000	135,889,600	80,588,000	37.1%
2004	**221,256,931**	**174,800,000**	**122,294,978**	**55.3**
2002	215,473,000	150,990,598	79,830,119	37.0
2000	**205,815,000**	**156,421,311**	**105,586,274**	**51.3**
1998	200,929,000	141,850,558	73,117,022	36.4
1996	**196,511,000**	**146,211,960**	**96,456,345**	**49.1**
1994	193,650,000	130,292,822	75,105,860	38.8

Year	Voting-age population	Voter registration	Voter turnout	Turnout of voting-age population (percent)
1994	193,650,000	130,292,822	75,105,860	38.8
1992	**189,529,000**	**133,821,178**	**104,405,155**	**55.1**
1990	185,812,000	121,105,630	67,859,189	36.5
1988	**182,778,000**	**126,379,628**	**91,594,693**	**50.1**
1986	178,566,000	118,399,984	64,991,128	36.4
1984	**174,466,000**	**124,150,614**	**92,652,680**	**53.1**
1982	169,938,000	110,671,225	67,615,576	39.8
1980	**164,597,000**	**113,043,734**	**86,515,221**	**52.6**
1978	158,373,000	103,291,265	58,917,938	37.2
1976	**152,309,190**	**105,037,986**	**81,555,789**	**53.6**
1974	146,336,000	96,199,020[1]	55,943,834	38.2
1972	**140,776,000**	**97,328,541**	**77,718,554**	**55.2**
1970	124,498,000	82,496,747[2]	58,014,338	46.6
1968	**120,328,186**	**81,658,180**	**73,211,875**	**60.8**
1966	116,132,000	76,288,283[3]	56,188,046	48.4
1964	**114,090,000**	**73,715,818**	**70,644,592**	**61.9**
1962	112,423,000	65,393,751[4]	53,141,227	47.3
1960	**109,159,000**	**64,833,096**[5]	**68,838,204**	**63.1**

Yet, memorizing a chart about how a proposed bill becomes law doesn't excite many young people. Schoolhouse Rock, the popular video series attempted to make learning this content more enjoyable through their songs and jingles, but the fact still remains: there is no substitute for experiential learning. When students visit the nation's Capitol and see legislation debated on the floor of Congress, meet with a lobbyist to understand how he or she represents the views of a segment of the population and hear how lawmakers dicker with each other to gain support for bills, they see the real face of government. They get an accurate picture of civics that is difficult to present in a classroom.

EDUCATIONAL TRAVEL BUILDS THE FOUNDATION THAT WILL ALLOW OUR STUDENTS TO SUCCEED IN A GLOBAL SOCIETY

In order for one to succeed in a global society, one must be able to function cross-culturally on multiple levels. In her Literature Review: studies of the impact of a travel-abroad experience (1984), Dr. Bettina Hansel examined the experiences of more than 8,000 secondary school students who participated in the AFS international exchange programs in 1983. She reports that Cigdem Kagitcibais' study of a 10-month program on student participants from Turkey showed that the world mindedness among the students increased and that authoritarianism and religiosity decreased. Further, Robert A.C. Stewart's work with 200 New

---

*Source 2008 election results: http://elections.gmu.edu/Turnout_2008G.html.

n.a. = not available. NOTE: Presidential election years are in boldface.

1. Registrations from Iowa not included.
2. Registrations from Iowa and Mo. not included.
3. Registrations from Iowa, Kans., Miss., Mo., Nebr., and Wyo. not included. D.C. did not have independent status.
4. Registrations from Ala., Alaska, D.C., Iowa, Kans., Ky., Miss., Mo., Nebr., N.C., N.D., Okla., S.D., Wis., and Wyo. not included.
5. Registrations from Ala., Alaska, D.C., Iowa, Kans., Ky., Miss., Mo., Nebr., N.M., N.C., N.D., Okla., S.D., Wis., and Wyo. not included.

Source: Federal Election Commission. Data drawn from Congressional Research Service reports, Election Data Services Inc., and State Election Offices.

Read more: National Voter Turnout in Federal Elections: 1960–2008 — Infoplease.com http://www.infoplease.com/ipa/A0781453.html#ixzz1JLRzOMzf

Zealand students who went abroad and their best friends showed a greater decrease in ethnocentrism than the latter group; his work, however, also showed that they became more conservative. Dr. Hansel's body of work also examined the findings of Norman Kauffman's study of Goshen College's (Indiana) trimester program on the personality development of student participants. Kaufmann's study found greater change than in other college students in: a.) a changed world view, b.) increased interest in the welfare of others and c.) greater intrapersonal personal development. The conclusions were that those students who travel abroad were likely to alter their views regarding the host country. The factors that contributed to a significant difference were length of stay, age, and the sex of the participant.

According to Elizabeth Reddin (2010), in 2000, researchers began an ambitious effort to document the academic outcomes of study abroad across the 35-institution University System of Georgia. Ten years later, they've found that students who study abroad have improved academic performance upon returning to their home campus, higher graduation rates, and improved knowledge of cultural practices and context compared to students in control groups. Redden also reports studying abroad helps, rather than hinders, academic performance of at-risk students.

According to Palmer (2003), the globe is shrinking today as never before. When students in today's schools graduate from college, they are more likely than ever to be working in a global community. They will need to understand the language, customs, geography, business climate, and habits of other nations. Certainly, some of this can be learned in the classroom, but what better way to truly understand the culture and habits of people from another country than to live in their homes for a week? What better way to learn their language than to speak it during a two-week tour of their nation? Is there a more effective way to start building an understanding of their business climate than to see how their stock exchange operates or speak with businesspeople of that country?

EDUCATIONAL TRAVEL COMPLETES THE LEARNING EXPERIENCE FOR STUDENTS INVOLVED IN THE PERFORMANCE ARTS

Music students can work hard all year in their classrooms, but they don't benefit from the complete learning experience without travel. Going to band, orchestra and chorus competitions, clinics, and exchange programs with other schools' music departments gives music students the opportunity to learn how to perform. These trips also help them build pride in their performances and give them incentive to work harder.

The same can be said for those students who participate in forensics, debate and chess, where day-long competitions at numerous sites throughout one's city, state and nation are par for the course. At a recent chess tournament, one school fielded thirty-two students in third through eighth grade. These thirty-two students were "held captive" in their thoughts and actions regarding chess from 8:00 a.m. until the completion of the awards ceremony at 3:00 p.m. During that time, team members met new friends from fifteen other schools, explored the grounds of the host school, and made plans for upcoming tournaments to be held at area museums, businesses and even waterparks. On this particular Saturday, this chess tournament was considered to be a small one!

Mind you, I have said nothing of the forty-five peers of the aforementioned chess team who are simultaneously "doing their craft" nearly one hour away at another venue: meeting new friends, performing, exploring and planning. For these students, educational travel becomes the motivation for being actively involved even on one's weekend.

EDUCATIONAL TRAVEL CAN BE THE SPARK THAT "TURNS ON" AN UNMOTIVATED STUDENT

No one is arguing that school board members adopt policies that replace instruction in mathematics and language arts with travel. But it makes sense to also provide educational travel opportunities to bring life to classroom lessons. Palmer (2003) has seen under-motivated students work harder and improve their academic performance after a travel experience. The values of student travel are numerous, and educational travel is part of a complete education.

According to Schenker (2007), children benefit greatly from being able to see what they are learning in class. Experience is the best teacher and by allowing students to see their classes come to life, an environment is created in which children will embrace their education. See, hear, touch, live and learn.

In addition to these many benefits of educational travel, Banes (2008) says "all children deserve the opportunities of educational travel". Improved knowledge of world geography knowledge and understanding of other cultures; language acquisition; improved self-confidence; and career opportunities as well as becoming more open-minded are a few of the many benefits she cites in her work.

Despite these many benefits of student travel, school board members still have many questions: Are these programs reputable? Should we take certain steps to ensure that travel is safe for the students who are our responsibility? Are there potential problems that can be overcome through advance planning? School districts can minimize these problems by investing time in studying travel options.

Or, they could simply find more teachers as dedicated, organized and passionate as Mark Horowitz to run their student travel programs. Student travel is a great opportunity for students to become lifelong learners and Mark Horowitz epitomizes lifelong learning!

CHAPTER

15 DAYS

15 days. Not studying from a textbook. Not watching films or a DVD for that matter. 15 days of living, breathing, and experiencing someone else's culture. It is unbelievable for many American students to have this type of experience with their classmates. Certainly not at the age of nine! But it is true. Although my 4th grade class of 1978 was not a part of the Denmark experience (the class of 1995 would be his first), I am able to speak about the experience with firsthand knowledge because I was fortunate enough to travel as a chaperone with the 2008 group, a group which included my oldest child. The experience from my perspective will be discussed in a later chapter. It was 15 days I will never forget, and I am sure the same could be said for the twenty-eight 4th graders who went on that trip.

An endeavor of this magnitude cannot be accomplished alone. Enter Ms. Lis Faerch, a Danish teacher who Mr. Horowitz had befriended. Ms. Faerch takes care of all the details on the other side of the ocean. She is a teacher at Dyssegårdsskolen, the host school in Denmark. Her perspective follows:

"In 1980 17 teachers from Milwaukee came to Odense, Denmark to teach English with the school's English teachers. Mark Horowitz came to stay at my house and teach with me for three weeks. We became friends. The year after that, he brought his wife Mary to Denmark. After that he has been on several occasions to visit. One time he called and asked if they could come for another visit and I, as always, said of course. Then he asked if he could bring 29 kids! There was a silence where I contemplated what that could entail. Then I said 'yes,' and that was the start of our programme. It was 1994.
The first year we did a lot of corresponding by snail mail. We sent Danish music which was popular that year translated into English and a lot of other stuff crossed the Atlantic.

When the Americans came we took all the students on all the trips. On other trips just the hosts (families with whom the American students live) and the Americans, which was a big mistake. First of all we were too many and secondly the rest of the classes felt left out.
My class wanted to visit the United States and we arranged with the parents to start saving up. The parents didn't think they should travel to the USA until 8th grade. After some time, the kids felt that the goal was too far out in the future so they didn't want to save all their savings for that trip.

Over the years we have made some changes to the programme so that we today think that we have the best programme for everybody.

Some years it has been more difficult than others to get enough hosts, but recently the programme has been so well-known among the 4th graders that we have had enough hosts. Every year I hold an orientation evening for the coming hosts but not many people turn up. Some hosts complain that the American kids are too young, but from my own experience as a host I don't think so. My own daughters had a wonderful time when they were 4th graders and so did the rest of the family. We had two girls staying and it was a very giving experience. Our daughters grew with the responsibility. It was great to watch. One girl kept in contact for some years and we visited her in Milwaukee, but then she moved. The other girl didn't keep in contact.

One of my daughters who had had an American staying stayed with Mark and Mary for a year when she travelled to the USA; she attended Riverside High School. One day she heard one of her classmates say that she could also say something in Danish. Gitte (pronounced "GEE TA") asked how come and it turned out that she had been in Denmark the same year that Gitte also had an American stay. Other persons told her they had also been in the programme and suddenly it dawned on me about 500 people in Milwaukee have been in Denmark through this program! That is quite amazing. It is also amazing to walk with Mark in Milwaukee and meet a lot of these people who all exclaim that it has been a life changing experience for their kids.

In 2009, it brought tears to my eyes on the evening of the farewell party. Karen Backes, who has been a student of Mark's, now came as a chaperone and as a student teacher. To see her with her Danish host was so nice. They couldn't say goodbye to each other and they have already visited each other several times.

There are so many Danish families who over the years have visited Milwaukee to see their 'American' I think it is such a big thing." And as they say, the rest is history.

Lis Faerch isn't the only Dane who has been greatly impacted by this endeavor. In the fall of 2010, in preparation for the 2011 excursion, Lis visited Milwaukee's Golda Meir School to talk to the American students about their upcoming European adventure. She brought with her Ms. Birgitte (pronounced "BER GEET") Bech, another teacher at Dyssegårdsskolen. Hearing that an American professor of education was producing a book about the Denmark experience, Ms. Bech was glad to share how this trip had impacted her as well. What follows are her dreams about coming to America:

DREAMING ABOUT COMING TO AMERICA

"When I was a little child, my Dad read a Danish poem for me called "Flugten til Amerika"/Flieing to America written by Christian Winther. The poem was about living in America and everything was better than living in Denmark! The poem taught me 'that in America candy grows on the trees and when it is raining the rain is soft drinks'.

Being a 5 years old child, I was wondering about how this country could be and I think that my own dream about 'Coming to America' started at that time. Being a teacher and for a period a parent at Dyssegårdsskolen, I have been a part of Mr. Mark Horowitz's program, hosting 4 parents and 2 children during the years. I have followed from the sideline all the trips Mr. Horowitz has been doing to Denmark during all those years and the program also gave me a great opportunity to realize my American dream.

I have now been visiting Milwaukee and the fourth grade at Golda Meir School 3 times, and during all the years I have gotten to know many people in Milwaukee – nice and wonderful people. It is always a pleasure to come to Wisconsin; people 'are fighting to see and to meet us' when we are here. The hospitality is amazing.

I think this program that Mr. Horowitz started in 1994 makes the world a little smaller and brings a better understanding between people. To me, making friendship across the world is to learn and respect other people with a different background and a different story than my own story. This American-Danish program gives the children at Golda Meir School and Dyssegårdsskolen a great beginning to start to build a friendship, a friendship that can last for a long time, maybe forever.

When I am visiting Milwaukee it is great to meet people around the town telling: I have been to Denmark with Mr. Horowitz and I am still in contact with my host. And in Denmark the children at Dyssegårdsskolen tell about how they have been to Wisconsin on holiday with their families visiting their American friends.

I went to church with some friends here in Milwaukee and at church I met a lady telling me: 'I have been to Denmark, my son has been to Denmark and we are still in contact with the family there'. When we are here in Milwaukee we hear that kind of stories almost every day – wonderful stories.

Well, my American dream came true thanks to this American-Danish program. I have got American friends that will last forever; we have many stories to share and I am so grateful for that. All of us who are or have been in contact with this program must be goodwill ambassadors for the future so the friendship between Golda Meir School and Dyssegårdsskolen can continue in the future.

It is very important in life that you go for your dreams. Sometimes you are so lucky that people cross your way and help you to realize that dream. Let us together go for this dream that the friendship between Golda Meir School and Dyssegårdsskolen still will grow."

BIRGITTE BECH, DYSSEGÅRDSSKOLEN, DENMARK

There is a reason why Denmark continues to receive number one status as the happiest country in the world. What other group of people would be kind enough to open their homes to American strangers for two weeks out of the year, disrupting their happy lifestyles to accommodate American children and their chaperones? Although Mark Horowitz is the driving force behind the Denmark experience of Room 23, make no mistake about it this program would not succeed if it weren't for the likes of the many Danish families who serve as hosts for the American children. Danish families (like the ones headed by Torben and Charlotte.) "We believe this program is an example of best practice that should be shared and leveraged with more schools both in the United States and in Denmark," said Charlotte and Torben, soon to become "new parents again" for my son Benjamin, who at the time of this writing is just two weeks away from departure! "We appreciate having had the opportunity to follow the program over the years." When my son arrives, he will be the third American the Kruse family has had the privilege of hosting.

The Kruse family reports that their own children take very seriously the role of hosting. "The kids are always very excited during the time leading up to the visit, no matter if it is an adult chaperone or a student. They want to take good care of our guests." For those of us who are thousands of miles away stateside, that's music to our ears!

Some families in Denmark have been so moved by the cultural exchange that they have felt compelled to write letters to the administration of Dyssegårdsskolen, the host school in Hellerup, Denmark. What follows is one such letter from a Danish mother encouraging the school's headmaster to continue the relationship. What is most encouraging about this letter is the fact that this Danish mother no longer has school-age children who will benefit from this program, yet she is adamant about its continuation:

> Dear Maj-Britt
>
> As the mother of two children who each have had an American staying this year and 3 years ago, I would urge that Dyssegård School continues this tradition.
>
> Not only does it give the children a unique chance to actually use their English skills, it also has been developing for them in many ways. They have learned what it means to be "a good host" that you have a responsibility to make your visitor feel welcome. They learn about other cultures in terms of everyday life, family, school, etc.. For me it has been especially important that children are realizing that Americans do not necessarily live the glamorous life that many Danish children get the impression from movies, TV, internet and other media. The Danish children also learn much about their own country to be with the American children who are extremely well versed in Danish history, culture and more.

Besides all the direct benefits that my children have had to have an American child living with them, it is quite clear to me that there are countless other common benefits. For example, the recent visit resulted in many relationships within the same class, and also across Dysegård School 4th classes. My daughter, who goes to 4.B made contact with a girl from 4.C and invited her home to us so they could Skype with their "Americans" who were friends. It has not only been actual physical visits have been fruitful. In the month before, many mailed and Skype together, thereby strengthening both oral and written skills.

There is also no doubt that it helps the children themselves to dare to let go and engage in communicating in a foreign language. You realize of course that they both understood and that they understand what the American says. And if not, well, you will ask again.

Parents Intra, telephones, etc. Have been on fire before and during the visit to arrange joint events, pickup at the airport, Tivoli Tours mm. which has certainly stimulated the community among both students and parents in the class. I would also like to stress that it was not only "host families" who participated in these events. Both "share-hosts", "friends", etc. were part of the events, so even children who have not had an American living with him, has been involved also in addition to what has been going on at school.

When I talk with friends, colleagues and family, and especially teachers in other schools about this visit, it is always the same reaction that follows. Enthusiasm, "jealousy" and great interest.

> Even though I have no more children who will benefit from having an American - although we hope for a return visit in eighth class, if the contact is still there - but I would really like to help upcoming 4th classes on Dyssegård School and their families to get the same opportunity that my children and I have had.
>
> I therefore hope that the school will find a way to continue Lis' beautiful and impressive work, so these visits will be continued as part of Dyssegård school's tradition and reputation.
>
> Many friendly greetings
> Susanne Michelsen

I wonder if Mark Horowitz realizes how many paths he has crossed and lives he has impacted?

For many of us who are teachers, we tend to use field trips as rewards or additions to the curriculum. It makes sense in a unit on animals to visit a farm or a zoo; however, what about when the field trip is the curriculum? How many of us have had that experience? Let me explain. The Denmark experience actually begins at the end of the student's third grade year. In May of each school year, letters are sent to all of the Golda Meir third grade students and their parents. The letter explains the purpose and organization of the program. Students and parents have the option of choosing to be in the program. Only those who ask to be in the program are put into it. Every year, there is a waiting list to get in to Room 23! For those who are chosen, Mr. Horowitz meets with the children and their parents shortly before the end of the school year to explain how the program works, answer any questions which the students and parents may have, and discuss fundraising. The cost of the trip is now about $1,600, inexpensive for a 15-day trip to Europe, but a lot of money for a school trip. Since

Golda Meir students come from a very diverse set of economic backgrounds, fund-raising is a necessity for the class.

During the summer, the children have the opportunity to begin earning money for the trip. Summer fund-raising events include a candy sale, a tulip bulb sale, and running a concession stand at the girls' state high school soccer tournament. The students are also given study CDs so they can begin to learn the Danish language. When school begins at the beginning of September, most children have already earned about one fourth of the money needed for the trip. Fundraising events, which continue throughout the school year, have included a pizza sale, a kringle sale, and a fruit sale. During the school year, classes do some preparation for the trip every day. This includes studying the Danish language and culture, history and geography; reading works by Danish authors, particularly stories by Hans Christian Anderson; and learning about the metric system, Danish foods, and songs. Since the class also spends approximately 30 hours in Amsterdam on the way home, the students become experts on artist Vincent Van Gogh as part of the trip includes a visit to the Van Gogh Museum in Amsterdam. Students also learn about Anne Frank and smart cars; the former is experienced through a visit to the museum in Amsterdam and the latter are visible throughout the city streets. No stone is left unturned in this 15 day experience. From the moment the American students touch down on European soil, learning begins!

Actually, learning begins way before that. Correspondence with their Danish friends begins during the fall semester. Students are assigned to a Danish host and begin corresponding via written letters, emails and on occasion through "skyping" when available. Each student and chaperone lives with a Danish host for the duration of the trip. Stateside, under the skillful direction of Mr. Horowitz, the American students begin to utilize their newly learned Danish speaking skills through conversations, math lessons and presentations. A good portion of the fall semester is spent immersed in the language. This is true learning!

When in Denmark, the students from Golda Meir simply become a part of their Danish family. If the family plays soccer (and a good number of them do), then the American student plays soccer. If the family travels on the weekend, then the American student travels on the weekend. It is still somewhat surreal to me that in April of 2008, on a blustery Friday afternoon, I stood on the grounds of Kronborg, a famous Danish castle that sits on the tip of Denmark and across the Oresund Sea my oldest daughter was traveling(let's be precise-shopping!) with her host family in Sweden! These moments are certainly not measureable on any standardized test of which I am aware; yet the significant learning that occurs on this trip is simply priceless and ought to be considered as model instruction!

If I have not emphasized this enough already, I do want to say that this experience, this trip, is truly what Stephen Covey would deem a 'win-win scenario'. Not only do the American students learn by having this experience, but so do the Danish students and their families. As a part of the 15 day experience, the Americans attend school with their Danish hosts. English is a class that is studied by the Danish. Everyone studies it at all levels in school in Denmark. So to have a real live English speaking student in your classroom for a week is a priceless learning opportunity for the Danish as well. The American students, in their learning, also become teachers! Everybody wins! What a fascinating way to learn!

As if traveling to Denmark wasn't enough for the students to get excited about learning, the trip concludes with a 30 hour tour of Amsterdam. "We use to say goodbye to our Danish hosts on the last day," says Mr. Horowitz, "but then the crying would last nearly 9 hours as we made our way back to the states. So, I made the decision to add a stop in Amsterdam!"

Who thinks like this?

"We now say good bye to our hosts on Day 14(there are still tears!), board the train to the Copenhagen airport and then travel to Amsterdam." This teacher wastes no time, for as soon as they land in Amsterdam, the group is connected to a tour guide and bus driver who for the next 20 hours or so provides transportation to a wooden shoe factory, a cheese factory, windmills, the Van Gogh Art Museum, a canal boat tour and the Anne Frank House! These young people are tired, but the learning never stops! Without having knowledge of the other 16 trips and their Amsterdam lodging accommodations, I cannot say for certain whether or not the 2008 group's hotel was the best. Suffice it to say, I have a hard time believing that any other year's group had a more breath-taking view than ours, as on our last night in Europe, I found myself standing with 28 American children on a sandy beach adjacent to our hotel on the North Sea!

I am a strong proponent of learning outside the four walls of the classroom; therefore, it should come as no surprise to you to hear me talk about the value of the experience outside of the classroom. As mentioned above, the American students become a part of the Danish family. Again, I count this as one of those surreal experiences to know that on any given day during those 15 days in Europe, approximately 30 American students were literally scattered across suburban Copenhagen and Amsterdam, immersing themselves in another culture. Does this have an impact on a child's learning and world? You bet it does! As evidenced by this anecdote I was privileged to experience while in Denmark: an African-American boy says quite seriously to his host mom "May I use the phone to call my grandmother?" The hostess, somewhat concerned, agrees, and overhears her American "son" say: "Grandma, I am just calling to let you know that I am not coming home ever! I love it here in Denmark and I want to stay here with my host family. I love you. Good bye!" Tears come to the eyes of this Danish mom. It is understandable. Because I was there, I had the privilege of reflecting on the anecdote. I knew there were MANY similarities between what this Danish family and this American boy were experiencing on a daily basis. I really believe there are many more forces out there that unite us as human kind than divide us. We just need to have the will to take the time and opportunity to figure these out. Mark Horowitz has!

And how about the impact on individual Danish families? For Torben and Charlotte, the soon-to-be parents of my own son when he travels in 2011, the experience has been very meaningful to them as well as their two boys Victor and William. "I learned better English and it is exciting to meet new people from other countries," said their oldest child Victor, who really enjoyed having a "big brother" so-to-speak when their family hosted a student teacher in 2008.

The Danish have a term called "hygge" and it is used to describe the sense of family, community and well-being that is so often found in their culture. Thus, it comes as no surprise to this author to hear their younger son William describe being a host family as "fun and cozy...you know, like our term 'hygge'." I am pleased to know that my son's new "brother" is looking forward to the experience!

"For the kids, this is a wonderful opportunity to practice their English skills, learn about other cultures, and get a broader perspective on the world", said Charlotte and Torben. "We can see how this helps give them a basic openness to meeting new people and wanting to engage with them to learn more about their lives and perspectives. In a global world, where many of their generation will either work in multicultural companies within Denmark or go abroad to study or work, these intercultural skills will prove invaluable. For us as parents, it is great to see our kids leverage this opportunity, and we get a lot of inspiration too."

'I've been thinking I could take my class overseas' is how Mary Horowitz describes the first rumblings she heard about the Denmark trip from her husband Mark. "He would come home and say things like, 'I'm not going to do it, but if I did, this is how I would do it!' This may sound crazy, but in a way, Mark's Denmark program is his way of contributing to world peace. What he has done has been to create one on one ambassadors. It's pretty hard to hate people that you know so well." Mary has had the pleasure of watching the Denmark experience grow from its inception. "Mark is a great planner. He makes it look effortless, but he probably works at his job about 60 hours a week. He believes in his kids." And thus the program succeeds.

"Mark is totally dedicated to teaching. His job is his life!" I couldn't agree with Mary more. What else could explain a teacher's decision to go ahead with a trip of this magnitude even during America's darkest hour? "I was concerned that he would lose his job that year", said Mary.

September 11, 2001 will be forever etched in history. The world did indeed come to a standstill on that ill-fated day. We know firsthand the devastating impact 911 had on travel so it is no surprise that the Milwaukee Public School system placed a moratorium on international travel. It would appear that the Denmark trip of 2002 would not take place.

But, as Mary Horowitz reports about her husband, "Mark never takes days off". And that would also prove to be true of his approach to the 2002 Denmark trip. "Mark stands up for his principles", said Mary. And when the dust settled in Mr. Horowitz's battle with the Milwaukee Public School District that year, the trip did occur thanks to the relentless efforts of this incredible teacher. He rallied the parents, utilized one of Milwaukee's finest law firms for legal counsel and basically did "whatever it took" to make that trip a reality for those students. This includes taking an unpaid leave of absence in order to travel with his students.

"When I visit my brother's classroom, I see a level of intensity that I do not see in other classrooms", said Mark's sister Susan. "I do not think this trip is for every kid, but for those families who do choose this classroom, I give them a lot of credit for sending their children. I have been a chaperone on this trip and what I want to let Room 23 parents know is that besides my brother, there are lots of people looking out for their children! This trip has a profound effect on kids and really helps them see that the world is not so scary."

The next time you open up a Webster's dictionary and look up the words "committed", "dedicated" and "amazing", you should see a picture of Mark Horowitz.

2008 Tour Group preparing stateside

Danish webmaster Neils Erik: one of the individuals responsible for maintaining the website that American parents may follow while the students are overseas.

2009 Tour Group arriving in Copenhagen

Danes waiting the arrival of the 2009 Tour Group!

2008 Tour Group: Abby and Madie in Milwaukee preparing for departure!

One of the wonderful host families in Copenhagen

CHAPTER

HE DOES WHAT? PARENTS' PERSPECTIVES

"I don't know if I can do it," said my wife, referring to the decision we were about to make regarding our oldest child's fourth grade placement. "Two weeks overseas? For a school trip?" I am sure that our household is not the only one to have had this discussion over the years. If you are privileged enough to have a child in a third grade classroom at Golda Meir School, then you have either made up your mind to not choose Mr. Horowitz's room for your child for any number of reasons or you seriously contemplate a decision to send your child to him for any number of reasons.

As I waited anxiously in Milwaukee's General Mitchell International Airport for the 2010 group to return, I was surrounded by parents who had just entrusted this teacher with their child for 15 days in Europe! As I write these words, I am still in awe as to who would possibly allow this to happen to/for their child?

What parent in their right mind would do this?

What were they thinking?

"We could not deny her this experience...this once in a life time opportunity," said a father standing near me. "It was fabulous," I overheard another parent saying, assuming he was referring to the firsthand accounts he was receiving from his child. Flowers. Balloons. Hugs. Pictures being snapped everywhere. Tired eyes. And yet one gets the impression that if they had it all to do over again, they would!

"I may have to go back every year," said 2010 chaperone Tina Kurth. Actually, I don't think she is kidding as Tina is the mother of twins who went on the 2008 trip with me. She believed in the trip so much that she volunteered to return with the 2010 group despite having no direct connection to students of that school year! I might also throw in that Tina will return during the summer of 2011 with her daughter. You see, in his free time, Mark Horowitz is also an under-13 girls soccer coach in Milwaukee, Wisconsin with the Milwaukee Kickers Soccer Club and he is planning to take his girls team to play and travel in Denmark!

Still another parent remarks: "We found out about the Denmark program through a friend who is a teacher who sent her son. It was a life-changing experience for their son and we wanted the same for our child. I don't even recognize my son at times because he is off studying Danish instead of doing other things that he normally would choose to do!"

"We are confident this will be a great trip, and are so happy that our daughter gets to have this incredible experience at such a young age", said Crystal, a mother of a 2011 traveler. Crystal continues: "The selection process was not hard at all for our family. I too was a student of Mark Horowitz's when I was in fourth grade, so I was excited at the prospect of knowing that my daughter would be sitting in the same classroom that I once did, and learning a lot of the same material that I did (Sounds a whole lot like something an author who sold his suburban home did to insure his child would hopefully have the Golda Meir and Horowitz experience)! I knew that Mr.

Horowitz did not use traditional textbooks for many of his subjects; instead he created his own curriculum on a much more advanced level than traditional fourth grade classrooms. I remember the high expectations he had for all of his students, and the calm manner he used when speaking to them. It is rare these days to find a teacher that can relate so well with children and be a mentor, friend, disciplinarian, and a role model all at the same time."

"Because I knew all these things coming in, it was like a gift to know of all the opportunities I was placing into my child's hands!" Well said, Crystal! Well said!

"Our daughter is handling things like normal so far. Because the trip is coming closer, we are coming up with ways to strengthen the connection between the United States and Denmark. We recently checked out a book from the library that we are reading as a family to learn more about Denmark. We will be putting together a scrapbook for her host family to give them an idea of what our daughter's life is like here in Milwaukee. We have purchased a photo album already for our daughter so she can put photos from her trip inside upon her return. We as parents are planning the packing and preparations for her sendoff and return. We will each write our daughter a letter to put in her suitcase, and will include photos of us that she can keep near to her while she is away. We would like to have a dinner with close family and friends before the big trip and welcome her home with a gathering the weekend after she gets back to the U.S. I have to admit, I am getting quite nervous as the trip draws nearer, but I am focusing on not letting it show so as not to send any bad vibes to our daughter."

Ah, the things we will do, the lengths we will go to insure our children's health and well being! I believe Mark Horowitz does the same!

"I was a little nervous," said Alex's mom, "but I think it is a great opportunity for my son. I think he may be a bit more nervous than I was!" Alex will travel with the 2011 group.

Is all of this anxiety and worry worth it? By the looks of things and by the sounds of all of the people I have interviewed for this book,

I would have to say the answer is "yes". "We have seen our daughter mature and be more independent and responsible," said Jean, another parent of a 2011 traveler. "We are so proud when we hear her explain the trip to Denmark. She has realized that true friendships can happen via emails and phone calls, not always just in person. She has realized that a 10 year old girl in a completely different country and culture has a lot in common with her. She has become more willing to try different food items. She has become engaged and excited about learning new things. Lastly, she has learned an appreciation of the unique and valuable experience of the Denmark trip."

She has a MPS teacher to thank for all of that! I need not remind the reader that none of the items Jean described in regards to her daughter's learning are tested on the Wisconsin Knowledge and Concepts Examination. Jean reported that both she and her husband were completely on board from the time they first learned about the opportunity when their daughter was in third grade. "We all wanted this for her and hopefully for our first grade son! There were absolutely no reservations on either our or our daughter's part at the planning stages. She continues to have no reservations, just pure excitement and anticipation of being with her new Danish friend in person. Both my husband and I are starting to become anxious as the reality of the trip is setting in. I am starting to get teary eyed, thinking that for two weeks she will be so far and that this trip is the first (of many) times she will be leaving us.

When I stop to think of being a parent and the short part of our children's lives they are with us, I am amazed. As parents, we 'control' or think we control our children's experiences from birth until early adulthood (college or work); we can protect them. To think that at age 10, we will have no control and be able to offer no protection over this experience is terrifying and exciting at the same time. I have such mixed emotions-mostly pride and excitement but also some sadness that this is the first sign of her growing up and being independent! I am not nervous as we trust her and Mr. Horowitz completely. He has done such an amazing job establishing trust with the students and families. We also trust her Danish family, the Kirkegaards, and feel that we have a special bond even though we have never met and only spoken a few times.

THIS IS A CHANCE OF A LIFETIME!"

I know the feeling. I am holding out for our K-4 daughter to experience the magic of Room 23 as well!

Whether it be purely coincidental or strategic, many of the children who end up in Room 23 tend to have at least one parent as an educator; such is the case in my situation. I can only assume that this fact serves to only strengthen the program's base of support. Doreen, whose son will travel in 2011, writes: "I am a diagnostic teacher at two schools in MPS. My perspective as an educator is the same as my perspective as a parent. This is a fabulous opportunity and experience! The amount of learning and growing up that has taken place has been such a wonder to see both as a parent and a teacher. The expectations have been high and seeing Alek and his classmates meet those expectations is really exciting!

Alek knew he wanted to go to Denmark and we agreed it would be an awesome experience. In fact, the possibility of going to Denmark was a big "selling point" for Alek when it came down to leaving his previous school and friends. Really, we were surprised at how many people seemed shocked that we would "let" our child go to another country. I don't know how many people have said that we are so brave. Not really, just couldn't pass up this opportunity".

The Denmark program changes people. And that certainly has been true for Doreen's son as well. "We have seen Alek really become more responsible regarding homework at any point. It used to be a long process each night to get the homework done. Now he's done with it before the rest of us even get home! Also, he has become more aware of his own strengths and weaknesses. He is less of a braggart about his strengths and more accepting of his own weaknesses. You know, he just really has grown up a lot this year!"

The 2011 group will mark the seventeenth consecutive year of the program. By now, the program has sustained roots both on Danish and American soil.

One group of parents had to be the very first ones to "trust the process!"

"I can do this by myself mom," were the words Suzanne recalls her daughter saying as they discussed the possibility of Suzie chaperoning that very first trip in 1994. "Heather was a mature child and my husband and I thought this Denmark experience would be the greatest growing experience we could offer our daughter."

And so there was no fear, no trepidation on the part of these two parents about sending their daughter overseas for the very first Denmark trip! "The trip turned Heather into an international citizen," says Suzanne (and the reader will hear more about this in the following chapter). "At the airport that day (the day they were leaving for Demark), there was no crying, neither by Heather nor her classmates. I remember there being a collective eagerness as no one really knew what to expect. This was not only a new adventure for the students, but for him (Mr. Horowitz) as well...and we were fine with that."

This sentiment would not necessarily be the norm. "We weren't quite convinced we wanted to go to Denmark," says Janet Carr, parent and chaperone of that first trip. "It could be emotionally hard in terms of homesickness and how much would the kids retain, not to mention the cost versus the value of the trip." But none of that deterred the Carrs from signing their son Adam up for Mr. Horowitz's classroom.

Said Janet: "He's the best...he's intense and there's lots of pressure to be successful. Mark Horowitz is dedicated to offering his students a well-rounded education of the highest caliber in all areas, including academics, humanities and the arts." What else could possibly explain why a teacher like Mark Horowitz would give a student like Adam French horn lessons the summer after having had Adam in his classroom? To encourage Adam's progress and his love for this common instrument that Adam continued to play until his college years.

"Having our child in Mr. Horowitz's classroom was born out of our desire to have our child have a world experience. The trip to Denmark is certainly an asset to Mr. Horowitz's classroom," Said Janet Carr. "He nurtured thinking outside of the box and creativity as well as the stretching of students' comfort zones and trying new things".

"It's not just about his taking kids to Denmark," said another parent who I interviewed for this book. "It's the level of expectations, the personalized approach to learning spelling, the computer programming and much, much more. In my opinion, Denmark is just the icing on the cake."

LIFE HAPPENS

Anyone who has had the privilege of being a parent knows that life happens and things don't always go as planned. So imagine being a 4th grader in Mr. Horowitz's class in 2006 and shortly before Christmas break, your parents tell you that your family is potentially going to be moving out of the city in a few months. This means you will be leaving your friends, your school...and in this scenario the once-in-a-lifetime trip that you had been working towards. "I was so mad", said Madie, the innocent bystander of "life happening."

Richard, Madie's father, explains: "We were living in Milwaukee, but I worked about an hour north of Milwaukee and the commute became very tiring. We really needed to move and I told my family that if the opportunity presented itself we would do so and it did. But, we were concerned about leaving Golda Meir and this wonderful opportunity for our daughter. As I recall, we wanted to talk to Mr. Horowitz about the situation and how it would affect Madie's participation before we finalized our plans. We were very supportive of Madie being in Mr. Horowitz's class. How could we deny her this opportunity? And now this might not happen."

"When Mr. Horowitz found out that we would be moving out of Milwaukee in January, 2006, he approached us and said 'She's still going. We'll figure out a way to still keep preparing her for the trip.' And, with those reassuring words, we felt much better about our move knowing that Madie would still be able to have this experience." It is some times said that you can't have your cake and eat it too, but one gets the sense that this family was able to do so!

And true to his word, Mark Horowitz found a way to keep Madie as a part of Room 23, even though she was now living and going to school about an hour north of Milwaukee: whenever her new school had a day off, Madie had a "day on" as arrangements were made to get her to Golda Meir School to be reunited with her Room 23 classmates; she was given compact discs to continue learning the Danish language, in addition to her "regular" homework; Madie's Danish host kept in touch with her through letters and emails; Madie's new class made and signed for her a farewell card which she still has today and if this wasn't enough to help her feel a part of Room 23 and prepare for this experience, Madie's new teacher used the experience as a geography lesson for the class by creating a poster entitled "Where's Madie?", in which they tracked Madie's travels through Denmark and Amsterdam, similar to the popular children's series Where's Waldo.

"At the parent meetings, I remember thinking 'this guy has it (the trip) planned down to every detail. I was very impressed with that and his track record," said Richard. At the end of the trip, one of the things that stood out to Charlene was the impact that technology had on the experience. "You have to remember that there was no YouTube in 2006 and the Denmark website was just coming into use. There I was in Wisconsin looking at the website and I could see pictures of my daughter saying farewell to her hosts, knowing that I would see her the very next day. It was remarkable and I was in awe!"

Madie's parents indicated she was already a confident young lady; however, the Denmark experience "brought her up another level. She became a world traveler, understanding Europe and being able to talk about health care and politics." I suppose that is what 15 days in another country can do for a young person!

HAVE SIBLINGS...WILL TRAVEL

And what about those families (such as mine) who decide to enroll multiple children in Mr. H's classroom? Enter Cynthia's story:

My daughter wanted to be in Mr. Horowitz's class from the very beginning of third grade. Initially we thought that this would be a great experience and wonderful opportunity. My husband was a little more hesitant than I was but went along nonetheless. He had spoken with a parent who didn't care too much for Mr. Horowitz which fed into some of his reservations. My daughter and I were pretty adamant about her going and my husband didn't want to be the spoiler. It was at the first meeting when we got our Danish tape and all of the summer work that the whole concept of what we were planning became quite scary. I didn't want to lose face with my husband, but I was getting very scared about sending my daughter to another country to people that I didn't know. I got resistance from some of my family and friends. It was a decision that we really talked and prayed about and had others to pray for wisdom for us. We did go back and forth whether this was the right decision or not. I talked to as many people as I could about their experience in Mr. Horowitz's class and all of them were positive. This helped, but there was still a lot of anxiety and doubt about sending my daughter to another country.

When Mr. Horowitz asked if I was still interested in chaperoning, a huge sigh of relief and excitement went through me. Now I was going on this great adventure with my daughter, how awesome is that? Although I heard other chaperones' experiences, I still didn't know exactly what to expect. I don't have a most memorable experience about Denmark. I remember the transformation in the kids after we left Mitchell Field and arrived in Minneapolis. They left crying and sad, but just a short time later the excitement of this experience took over and their faces just showed it. They were ready for this. I was amazed at how much the kids knew about Denmark and Danish culture, Van Gogh, castles and the Vikings. I had the best family and the relationship I was able to establish with them was great. One night I was talking with my host family about Mark making this trip year after year and how this would start to get boring. After the first trip we all took as a class, I realized it was not about Mark coming to these places year after year but for him it was about these students coming here for the first time and their experience. He is the ultimate teacher, because his focus is always on the children and what they are learning. He was always telling them to look around, see what's different or the same. I remember sitting in the restaurant in Amsterdam at a table with 3 ten year olds. We had the best conversation, they had great manners and I truly enjoyed this dinner party.

This experience has given my daughter a more global perspective on everything. I think she is not limited to what she sees but knows there are a lot of opportunities available to her. She has talked to me about moving to France to be a professional ballet dancer. She seems more mature and just more open-minded about new experiences.

My younger daughter is now a student in Mr. Horowitz's class. This child is very shy and quiet and I think this experience will have a different impact on her but definitely a positive one. I want her to travel to Europe and have the same kind of experience her sister had. I think she will really grow and mature, plus now that she has met my host family this summer she is more excited about going.

I think Mark Horowitz is one of the most dedicated teachers my children have had. I personally like his old school style of teaching. I think it works for him because he truly wants the children to learn and he pushes them (and parents too) to achieve high goals. He definitely is in a very elite class of teachers in my life and the life of my children."

Not only will Susan Odegard send multiple children to Denmark as a part of Mr. Horowitz's class, she herself went to Denmark twice as a part of the program; The first time as a student teacher; the second time as a mom.

"As a student teacher, I learned an enormous amount from Mark Horowitz! It's not something they can teach you in a methods course. I believe you have to be out and about with veteran teachers to learn their little tricks. Mark Horowitz is old school and I liked it. He had kids working at their own paces, he set such a good example for students by being prepared and disciplined and presented himself with such a quiet style. One of the most important things I learned from him is you don't have to yell to get students' attention. I rarely heard him yell.

It was apparent to me during my first weeks of student teaching that my own children did not have any options for fourth grade other than being in this man's classroom." And so Susan and her husband decided to apply to Golda Meir School for their children, eventually requesting a fourth grade placement in Mr. Horowitz's classroom. Susan said her son thoroughly enjoyed the Denmark experience. "He came back taller and older. When I went as a chaperone, all of the students seemed to have matured. I saw it! I was there! There was a sense of accomplishment. For my own son, he had to come out of his shell and fall into the rhythm of his host family. This Denmark experience...my husband and I couldn't have given that to him."

Susan went on to report that her son talks to his young sister "all the time" about what she can expect when she travels to Denmark in 2011: 'This is going to be your best year of school. *I have never learned more from any teacher.'* "My son, as well as I, has a deep respect for Mr. Horowitz," said Susan. "I think we sell our kids short in terms of what we expect of them. To see students held to such high standards by a teacher was new to me. Another thing I really liked about Mr. Horowitz is that he talks directly to the students during parent-teacher conferences. After all, the event is about them, why shouldn't he?"

I could not agree with you more Susan!

"It blows your mind," said Susan, "to think that he is doing this for his students. It's magical how he brings kids along. Usually it's the parents who have the hardest time with the program! However, my husband and I want to raise our children to be global thinkers and by placing our children in Mr. Horowitz's classroom, we gave them the opportunity to accomplish this. *This is the kind of teacher every kid should have for at least one year of his or her life!*"

Susan's last comments reminded this author of an email exchange he once had with educator/author Alfie Kohn, a critic of our current public education system. His works, at least among my preservice teacher candidates, ruffles feathers because he asks us to not just think outside of the box when it comes to classroom organization, management and teaching, but rather to point inwardly and dismantle the box altogether, all the while working towards the creation of a new box.

After reading his *Beyond Compliance to Community,* my teacher education students wanted to know Mr. Kohn's thoughts on the following question: It takes a village to raise a child, but what if you don't work in a village that shares that mentality? Or, what if a significant part of the village is absent (parents) from the child's education? As controversial as Alfie Kohn may be, I gained a lot of respect for him as a result of his a) taking the time to respond to my question and b) for the content of his response.

Kohn responded "creating a caring classroom community(or for that matter, a place that is more about exploring ideas than memorizing forgettable facts and raising scores on bad tests) is obviously much easier when you have the support of your colleagues and when kids are getting the same basic messages throughout the school and home. When that is not the case, you do what you can to invite parents and other educators to reconsider their practices and premises. In the meantime though you do what you can with the opportunities you have. *In a single year and even in a single class, kids can be profoundly affected by being treated with trust and respect* and by being asked to reflect together quite explicitly on the differences between a "working with" and a "doing to" environment. They may be plunged back into bribes and threats when they leave you, but you've given them a gift that no one can take away: the knowledge that it could be otherwise".

Golda Meir School is a special place, with special students and special teachers. It is quite obvious to me Mark Horowitz and his colleagues have given the children and families of Golda Meir School a gift no one can take away: the knowledge that education can and should be lived beyond the walls of the classroom.

CHAPTER

FROM THE MOUTHS OF BABES

So what do the children think of this teacher and this once-in-a-lifetime experience, especially those who were on that very first trip? "We had something special," said Heather, now 26 years old, sitting across from me with her Denmark scrapbook neatly intact even after all these years. Although she doesn't remember the very first days in Mr. Horowitz's class, she did say she remembers thinking "Doesn't everybody do this?"

No, Heather, every teacher does not care for and prepare their students for success as Mr. Horowitz does. You did have something special, just like every child who has had the privilege of being a member of Room 23 throughout all these years. When asked what her thoughts about Mr. Horowitz were, Heather said:

"He is absolutely one of the best teachers I have had! Mr. Horowitz made learning exciting. My vocabulary expanded when I was in his room. To this day, I remember some of the new words I was introduced to: sheath, obese, rotund."

"He gave me an international mindset!" Wow! Wouldn't it be great if every American student could say this about his or her teacher? "I hadn't traveled outside of the country at that point in my life. Although it was a new and somewhat scary experience, traveling to Denmark really bound us as a class. This trip made international travel within your reach." Since her first international trip in 1995, Heather has traveled to France, Iceland, England, Canada, Mexico, Ireland, Scotland and Turkey. And to think that she has a Milwaukee Public Schools teacher to thank for cultivating her interest in travel!

"He's (Mark Horowitz) just a man who crafted his art." No, Heather, I would say he is continuing to craft his art even to this day! That's what the great ones do-they simply continue to get better.

"It's a scary thought that someday he won't be there," said Heather, with a sorrowful look on her face. Yes, Heather, I agree with your statement. I also cannot imagine Room 23 without Mr. Horowitz.

"We had something special."

Yes, you did!

Heather called it special. Others saw it differently. "Why are we so lucky?" Adam recalled thinking during his beginning weeks as a fourth grader in Mr. Horowitz's class during the 1994-1995 school year. "The kids who came before us were pissed! It was ridiculous to think that this group of nine and ten year olds would be traveling to Europe!"

As Adam and his classmates would soon discover, there was nothing ridiculous about it at all. It was really going to happen and Adam would be one of the first to travel to Denmark.

"Breakfast in Denmark was amazing!"(I would have to agree with you on that one Adam!) "I remember having chocolate on bread. I remember the walking tour of Copenhagen and all of the beautiful architecture. It was cold that day, but it didn't matter; we were having great fun and learning!"

"The way in which he did this (got us to learn) was very inspiring to me!" said Adam. I will return to the idea that those things that are really important in life are usually not tested on standardized tests.

What struck me the most about my conversation with Adam was his vivid memory of Mark Horowitz's high level of expectations for students, a level that still remains high to this day. "Mark Horowitz was one of the best teachers I have ever had. There was a parental strictness about him that was amazing. He somehow was able to be a strict disciplinarian and also foster our creativity."

In listening to Adam's accurate portrayal of Mr. Horowitz- I was reminded of my days as an education undergraduate student listening to my professors talk about students really wanting structure in their lives; therefore, it was incumbent on us as teachers to have effective classroom management. My guess would be that these professors were talking about becoming the type of teacher that Mr. Horowitz has become!

Adam continued by saying this about Mark Horowitz: "He would challenge us. He would make us figure it out for ourselves... when I got an A+ from him, it really made me feel special. He really asked so much from us as fourth graders!"

He asked so much of us...

Are there any greater words a parent would want to hear about his or her child's teacher?

"Mr. Horowitz let us go as far as we were able to go," said Adam. "There were no bounds in terms of his expectations."

There were no bounds in terms of his expectations...

OK, I believe perhaps I have found those greater words!

"Mark Horowitz is my favorite teacher of all time", said Caroline, another member of the first group of "Danish Pioneers." "I was lucky enough to be in his class the first year of the trip and I would be delighted to contribute to this book in any way I can!" When a 26 year old young woman says someone is her favorite teacher of all time, I believe it is safe to say she has contributed to the book immensely! Caroline went on to say the Denmark trip "was a life-changing experience and I'm so thankful I was able to be a part of it. Please let me know how I can pay tribute to this wonderful man and his Danish adventure..."

"Mark Horowitz has high expectations for his students," said Karen Felder, a former student and student teacher of Mr. Horowitz. "He is inspirational and helps students rise to the challenges he presents. Mark is strict when it comes to student responsibilities but also has a great sense of humor and allows for time to have fun in the classroom". And what about the classroom climate this incredible teacher creates for his students? Karen said, "I remember 4th grade as the only year in my school career that I considered every one of my classmates to be a friend. We all worked and played together, even if we didn't always get along, regardless of gender, religion, race or ethnicity". That is quite a compliment to such an inspirational teacher! Brittany's words also speak volumes as to what a great teacher Mr. Horowitz is. "In fourth grade, I went to Denmark with my classmates. It was my first time travelling without my parents and staying in a foreign country for two weeks. The prospect was quite intimidating as a nine year old but the trip was run so flawlessly that I could focus on my time in Denmark".

In this fast paced world, it was hard to track down the many number of students and/or chaperones who have benefitted from this life changing teacher and international experience. If one really stops to think about it, the numbers present a fascinating story: 16 years (and counting!). 30 students each year. A minimum of 6 chaperones per year. That's well over 500 people who have walked a mile in someone else's shoes all because of one teacher's passion for teaching and learning. Although I didn't connect with as many people as I would have liked, those who I did find were more than willing to share their stories.

MADIE'S STORY

The reader has already been introduced to Madie, probably the only student throughout the Denmark experience who has had an entire bulletin board devoted to tracking her adventures! "I was afraid I would be homesick," says Madie, who traveled in 2006. "But, there were so many things to do there that I never had the chance to be homesick! My fondest memory of the experience was visiting the outdoor museum, The Frilandsmuseet. We pretended like we lived there. We all played together. It didn't matter that we were from different countries. We just played!"

Echoing the words of her parents, Madie said "The Denmark experience made me grow up. I skipped a whole level of maturity by being in Mr. Horowitz's class. He prepared us for the many cultural differences we would experience. The way I eat now is the way I was taught how to eat by Mr. Horowitz. I don't know any other way to do so!"

"Mr. Horowitz was a strict teacher…and I liked that. You're either on his good side or on his bad side. I suppose it is terrifying if you are on his bad side!"

I am sure the Denmark experience will always remain with Madie, as not only has she kept in touch with her host family, but in June of 2009, her host family came to the United States to visit. "They matched us so incredibly well," said Charlene, Madie's mom. "The host mom and I believe that we could have been best friends had we grown up together".

And to think that Mark Horowitz played a small part of that!

"In high school, when I talk with my friends about what I was able to experience as a fourth grader, they get wide-eyed!," Given that there is a Denmark, Wisconsin only minutes from where Madie now lives, one can only imagine how wide-eyed her friends must get when they find out it is Denmark, Europe!

"Denmark was great! You don't want to leave after those 15 days. At first you can't imagine going. Then you can't imagine leaving! I have never had another teacher like Mr. Horowitz. He never really talked down to us. He talked with us...he knew how to reassure us that this trip could be possible."

NATALIE'S STORY

"Mr. Horowitz is a great teacher. He is strict yet fun. I found that the way he teaches made me take in more information than I do some times in my current classes now."

In 2007, Natalie traveled to Denmark. "I have a lot of memories," says Natalie, now age 13. "One was when we went to the queen's garden and ate there. Another is when I stayed with my host family. We would watch some Danish shows that we have in America that they had in Denmark. I also remember the school ...the school had this big staircase that you would use to get in and out and I loved it!"

Natalie says the Denmark trip was a great thing and it helped her learn about people with different cultures. Standardized testing aside, isn't this the goal of education? Shouldn't it be? "The Denmark trip had influenced my life greatly, I think. I learned a lot about the wars in Denmark, which is one of the countries you don't hear about in the history textbooks. I learned how the Danish used to knock the smell of the dogs the Nazis used and when people talk about things like that, I know about it. I also got to see how people that live in places other than America are similar and different.

ANDREW'S STORY

In 2007, it was probably free; even though it probably wasn't much to write home to mom about. I am referring to airplane food, one of those "make shift" delicacies, especially on a long international flight. But don't tell that to Andrew, one of Natalie's classmates, who indicated that airplane food was one of his memories of the Denmark trip.

Different strokes for different folks!

But no worries-Andrew also rattled off: playing the trivia game on the plane, going to the Danish school each day, visiting the

Vincent Van Gogh Museum, and crying on the day they left Denmark were some of his favorite memories.

I understand. I experienced this first hand myself just one year after Andrew. I suspect it is a commonplace occurrence with these trips.

"The Denmark trip brought me to a whole new academic level," said Andrew. "Since the trip I have matured in bounds and found love in traveling."

Let me just take a moment to make sure I have the facts right:

- A 13 year old boy, who can reflect back on loving airplane food
- Crying because he had to return home
- Being taken to a new academic level because of this trip
- Who now says he has matured in bounds, thus finding a love for traveling

One cannot write a more perfect script than this!

Andrew's recollection of Mr. Horowitz was that he was "funny, strict but fair and smart." "Mr. Horowitz opened my eyes to the world as a whole, and allowed me to have the best school year ever." In addition to learning Dansk for the international experience, Andrew recalled numerous ways that this spectacular teacher left an impressionable mark on him that school year. "I remember Camp Silverbrook, learning cursive and finishing program 20," the latter a reference to an independent project whereby students write computer programs using the BASIC language. Students set their own goal regarding how many programs they will complete during the school year.

A QUALITATIVE LOOK AT PAST YEARS

What follows is a qualitative reporting of the experiences of the classes of 1999 and 2005. Their words are presented verbatim as obtained from reflective essays that Mark Horowitz has collected over time. What I have tried to do is to identify some common themes throughout each class' reflections. I understand that there is no way that a collection of reflective essays could ever gain favor in the eyes of state departments of education or instruction as a viable tool to determine whether or not students are learning, growing and making progress in their schools. However, there is growth and understanding in the words of these nine and ten year olds; a wisdom beyond their chronological age-knowledge of matter that will never be measured by a standardized test. We can only hope that the collective experiences of these fifteen day international fieldtrips will someday be measured by the individual acts of service and love and the random acts of kindness delivered by these young people on humanity! Perhaps they will pay it forward in their lives just as Mr. Horowitz has done for them.

1999: THE LAST GROUP TO TRAVEL IN THE 20TH CENTURY!

As I read the words of these pioneers and reflected on their thoughts about living in a foreign land, three words came to my mind to summarize their experiences: Emotional. Educational. Transformational.

EMOTIONAL

- "My trip was full of love, laughter and wonder...it will probably be the best thing that ever happened to me."
- "I was very sad when we were living(leaving) to go to Amsterdam…I tried not to cry, but I did…so was my host's brother…"
- "I liked the sense of security in Denmark. There is not as much violence and people trust people…"
- "My trip to Denmark was really exciting. When I first left home I was happy, sad, scared and worried all at the same time. After I got on the plane, I felt excited! When we got to Detroit, I felt like calling home. When we were in Amsterdam, I felt happy, excited, and afraid at

the same time. I got use to it after awhile. I got to love and care about my Danish family. I felt sad and responsible at the end. I cried really hard. When I got back to America, I talked a lot about Denmark. I feel responsible because I know my mom doesn't have to remind me to do some things!"

- "When it came to leaving, I almost couldn't. Almost everybody had mixed feelings..."

EDUCATIONAL

- "I think the trip was valuable because we got to study another culture and way of life."
- "I learned that people who are different can be very, very nice..."
- "It was so fun, it didn't seem educational!"
- "My host family did almost anything I asked of them... they made sacrifices for me..."
- "When we made it to Denmark, I was so happy I had a grin from ear to ear! My host was so shy, just like me. In the middle of my stay, I realized that we were so much the same but different. I liked being with someone different from me. Next time I travel I won't be scared!"
- "I learned to try new things..."
- "This trip didn't seem educational to any of us, because it was so fun! But, it was (educational)."

TRANSFORMATIONAL

- "Denmark changed me in many different ways...because of Denmark, I am not as shy as I used to be. At first I was scared, but by the end of the trip, my excitement had overcome my fear!"
- "I learned a lot but most importantly I became more independent."

- "We got to live on our own, make the rules, spend our own money…it was a part of growing up. I am more grown up now that I went on that trip."
- "Now after going to Denmark, I wish to go back and learn more of their language."
- "Denmark was a very good experience for me and it made me like travel even more….it made me want to try more things in life!"
- "We also gained new friends for life if you choose to remain friends. The first two days I was a little homesick. After awhile I was too busy…"
- "…then when I got home I felt more grown up like my parents. I also felt special because not every day does a kid in the fourth grade go to Europe. I THANK MY TEACHER A LOT BECAUSE I MIGHT NOT HAVE BEEN SO NICE AND NOT HAVE TAKEN 28 KIDS TO DENMARK!"

I believe the reflections of these two girls from the 1999 class truly sum up the totality of the Denmark experience for me. Kalarose wrote: "Denmark is a beautiful place. I didn't feel sad that much when I left but I felt fine and nervous at the same time. That changed quickly when I reached Denmark. I was excited and interested! I like Denmark and I will always remember Denmark even though it was a short time. Even though we've been to Denmark we could forget how lucky we were to go. That could be the only time I get to go to Europe at all. I think that I am lucky to be able to go to Denmark and I will always remember this trip of a life time."

I have a hard time believing Kalarose will ever encounter a question about life-changing experiences on her SAT or ACT test in future years…

Ashley's essay: "…As I got through the airports, I began to change. When I met my host, I wasn't sure I was going to like this place. But that made me stronger for Amsterdam and the rest of the trip. Being away from my family made me more independent. I have changed because of this trip. Though I still love my parent and cat, I don't need them as much. Speaking for the whole class now, I think we all became more mature and independent."

I wouldn't doubt it for a second Ashley!

2005

One can imagine the enormous effort required to keep a program of this magnitude running year after year. Through many conversations with Mark Horowitz, I have come to understand the various obstacles and hurdles a teacher has to overcome to launch and sustain a program such as the Denmark experience. It is quite the undertaking and I am sure there are low points when Mr. Horowitz might pause and reflect on whether or not to continue the efforts year after year. The thoughts of the class of 2005 provide an insight and perhaps a shot in the arm-a boost if you may-for anyone wondering whether or not this fifteen day adventure is a valuable and worthwhile experience.

- "I hope the Denmark program will continue. This year I got a new friend from it...Kim...I email Kim weekly and we send stuff every three months or so."
- "The Denmark trip builds friendship between kids for life. Its fun meeting new people trying new foods and hanging out in new places."
- "The most important reason to keep the Denmark program going is making life-long friends. Now I know two languages!"
- "The Denmark trip helps children learn about how everyone in the world is equal and should be treated that way. I have made life long friends."
- "It gave me a chance to have a life long friend from a different country. We are talking about having my host come to America or I might go back to Denmark."

- "One thing I learned on this trip was how to speak a different language which is a valuable lesson. I now have a life long friend."
- "The experience I had was a once in a lifetime chance for me to meet friends forever."
- "The reason we should continue the Denmark program is because it is an amazing and once in a life time experience. You learn to appreciate other cultures and you learn that not everything that's different is wrong. If you participate in this program, you will most likely have a friend for life."

In America, we have a popular game called 'Simon Says'. In 2005, Simon (from Mr. Horowitz's class) says: "The reason of why we should keep the Denmark program running is because not only the Americans learn, but so do the Danes." What's good for the goose... "We should keep the Denmark trip going because as a fourth grader at Golda Meir School I benefited in that I learned that people are people just like us and if everybody learns that all around the world there would be peace.

Imagine: every fourth grade class in the world taking two weeks out of their school year to experience what the Golda Meir students experience! I do believe the world would be a better place!

It has been my experience thus far that every group of students who has traveled to Denmark through this program has had at least one or two students whose essays or thoughts truly speak volumes about the importance of maintaining this opportunity for students. In 2005, that honor went to the words of Maya who said: "All kids should have this opportunity but unfortunately that isn't possible. If we want a better future we should make sure all kids know how to respect."

In some respects, Maya's right. The truth hurts sometimes! All kids should have an opportunity like this. Where I differ from

Maya is in her statement that it isn't possible. There are two ways that giving all kids this opportunity is possible. We can replicate Mark Horowitz across this vast world of ours.

Or, we can simply hope that all teachers coming out of pre-service programs set high expectations of themselves and their students in such a way as to create an environment for learning outside of their four walls, in such a manner that allows them to push themselves and their students to achieve their maximum potential!

Maya, I honestly do not know which solution is more realistically obtainable...

Had more students responded, it would be easy for me to include literally hundreds upon hundreds of wonderful stories from the many American children who have benefited from this program. But what about the kids across the ocean? How do they perceive the program? Although I was not able to hear from as many of them as I would have liked, I would have been remiss to not share Cecilie's story. She took the time to respond to my request for information and for that I am grateful. Her words also show how intricate and complex a program like this can be. For this, I am truly grateful because it provides us with a great perspective.

"In 2002 I hosted an American girl and her big brother. Their mother, who had come too, was hosted by one of the Danish teachers. When I was in 2nd grade I remember how me and my classmates walked around school asking for the American students' autographs. We were all looking forward to when it would be our turn to host an American student in the 4th grade. In general the whole school was always very excited to have them.

I had already been to the States for one month one or two years before we had the American kids coming to live with us, so I already knew quite a lot about American culture. And on the surface Denmark and USA have a lot in common - as the rest of the Western world Denmark has been highly influenced by American culture.

I wouldn't say, though, that my experience with the Denmark Program has impacted my life or my thoughts about America or Americans. These kids aren't the only source we have of American culture. We learn about American culture in a million different ways - TV, films, news, etc., etc. And when I was younger my parents told me how they had only been kids and that America is a very varied nation. On the other hand, I could imagine that I and my family have impacted the two Americans kids' thoughts about Denmark and Danes since we're probably the only or one of few sources they have of Danish culture."

Consider Nanna's experience: "In fourth grade I participated in the exchange program as a host. Today, in 2011, I am 21 years old and quite often I find myself thinking back at that particular exchange program. In many ways, it has shaped my life and it is hard to imagine what my life would be like if I had not participated.

I hosted D'Laney in 4th grade and we kept in touch until D'Laney came back with Mark Horowitz as a junior chaperone. When I was in 8th grade, I travelled to Milwaukee during the summertime to see and experience how D'Laney lived. We kept in touch after that visit and when I was 15 years old, I participated in the Rotary Youth Exchange Program, where I was so lucky to spend a year in Illinois attending high school and living with an American family. While living in Illinois, I often visited D'Laney and her family whom soon became like a second family to me. I would never have gone on this year-long exchange if I did not participate in the exchange program created by Mark Horowitz. This program between Golda Meir School and Dyssengardsskolen opened my eyes to the world and taught me how to better understand foreign cultures. If everyone in the world participated in an exchange program like the one created by Mr. Horowitz, the world would be a better and more peaceful place. To me, it is very valuable knowing that I have friends from other cultures and countries".

2008: A SPECIAL YEAR

In 2008, the Denmark trip took on a special significance for this author. I was afforded the opportunity to travel alongside the group as one of five chaperones. My oldest child, Abigail, would be among the twenty-eight fourth graders traveling to Denmark in 2008. I honestly do not know who was more excited, me or her! At some point during the school year, Mr. Horowitz pulled my daughter and me aside and asked us the million dollar question.

"There will be five travel groups. What I need to know is whether or not Abby would like to be in your travel group?" I know the answer I would have chosen for her, but I believe in giving students voice as much as possible and so I allowed Abby to make that decision.

"I'd like to be in a different travel group than my dad," my daughter responded without hesitation! The answer did not surprise me. In fact, it was the answer I had hoped she would have given. And from that moment on, I had the incredible fortune of watching not only my oldest child, but twenty-seven other fourth graders grow up in front of my very eyes. As these young people have expressed so eloquently throughout this chapter, it was emotional, educational, transformational and I did indeed create life-long friendships, a second family if you will!

What really stood out to me about the 2008 group was their respectfulness of one another, of their hosts and most importantly of their teacher, Mark Horowitz. Their essays also talked at great length about how this trip was life-changing, a once-in-a-life-time opportunity and an educational experience they would never forget; however, what I would like to reflect on about this great group of students is their very evident sense of gratitude for the amount of time and preparation that Mr. Horowitz puts into organizing the Denmark trip. The following excerpts are from their essays:

- "...thank you for giving your own time and lunches to work on our trip"
- "Thank you for organizing this wonderful trip...you

made us have a new friend from a different country"

- "If you weren't our teacher this trip probably wouldn't be possible...thank you also for giving up your time to work on the trip. You must have given up a long time each day to work on the trip"
- "This trip has taught me so much about the world, cultures and friendship...just making international friendships was incredible...you're the reason this trip was possible. We learned Danish and we learned (most importantly) to be SMITS-Sophisticated Mature International Traveler. I learned to be open-minded and that friendships last forever"
- "You planned everything so well...the friendship I made in Denmark was priceless. You can't buy it!"
- "Dear Mr. Horowitz...thank you so very much for arranging this giant trip for us. It's almost unbelievable that you've done this for 14 years with fourth graders, and you can also speak the language very well. Thank you for arranging the flights and everything. Tak!"

There is always one student who hits the nail right on the head when it comes to defining this teacher and this experience. Ironically enough, the 2008 winner of this award was also a student in my travel group. Here is Zane's year end reflection on the experience:

Dear Mr. Horowitz,

Thank you for taking your time and plans aside for our trip. This was a life-changing experience. My favorite part was Tivoli. *I'm curious about how you have enough time to help us with computer programs and plan simultaneously.* I hope that you never stop this field trip and all my siblings can experience it.

As a father of four, with one of them yet to be accepted at Golda Meir, not to mention being accepted into Mark Horowitz's class, I could not agree more with Zane's comments. I too am curious as to how you have enough time to do all that you do for the students. I also hope Mr. H. never stops this experience.

I mentioned earlier that 2008 was a special year because of the personal connotation of the trip. How often do a father and daughter get the opportunity to travel internationally with the latter's elementary teacher and peer group? It was truly an unforgettable moment in time. But that wasn't the only reason it was unforgettable.

"HOUSTON (MINNEAPOLIS), WE HAVE A PROBLEM"

Milwaukee to Minneapolis. Minneapolis to Amsterdam. Amsterdam to Copenhagen. That was supposed to have been the route for our group that year. The flight to Minneapolis was a very quick 50 minutes. And I will never, ever forget the descent into Minneapolis. The kids were jovial and talking about the trip and you could see the excitement building. Then Mr. Horowitz turned around and said to me "We have a little bit of a situation going on". Given that we were only in the air less than one hour and I did not feel any turbulence nor did we have any meals so it could not have been food poisoning, I could not imagine what the "situation" was. I was not prepared for the words that would then come out of Mr. Horowitz's mouth. "One of our chaperones left his passport and the passports of the six students in his travel group in the Milwaukee airport."

Guess whose daughter was one of those six students?

Word began to spread like wildfire about the "situation", and I am not referring to the Jersey Shores! It was 8:00 p.m. Our flight for Europe was leaving at 9:30 p.m. The people at KLM airlines in Milwaukee had found the passports, but the next flight out of Milwaukee to Minneapolis would not be until 10:00 p.m. And seven of our "family" members did not have the necessary documentation to continue the journey. Like a balloon being plucked with a stick pin, the jovialness and excitement quickly turned to anxious faces; even some tears began to roll down nine and ten year old cheeks. And as a chaperone and a father, even I wondered how in the world this "situation" would be rectified.

Even trying to recreate the experience for the reader right now is proving difficult. How do you explain what could have been a dream deferred? 6 children who were literally homeless; 22 of their peers who didn't know when they would be reunited with their classmates; 1 chaperone who felt absolutely horrible (there is really no other way to describe it); 1 chaperone who had to make a different and difficult decision for obvious personal reasons; parents who had to be notified; and 1 veteran teacher who showed incredible poise and grace under fire.

Mark Horowitz is a risk taker. Those who are successful in life, no matter the endeavor, are risk takers. While many who may have found themselves in our "situation" may have folded under pressure (myself included), this veteran risk taker did not. While Mark Horowitz already had, and always will have my undying support as the best teacher ever, what I witnessed that day from 8:00 p.m. until 9:30 p.m. can only be described as strokes of pure genius.

One of the first things Mr. Horowitz did was to calm the group of 6 students, and his use of humor could not have been more timely. I do not remember exactly what he said, but I can tell you that all 6 students laughed and had smiles on their faces. I do remember him saying the following to the group: 'Now remember, you all are SMITS, and these things will happen. Because you are ready for this trip, you will be ok. Here is the plan: Tonight you and your chaperone will stay here in Minneapolis at a local hotel. In the morning, you will get up early and come to the airport to retrieve your passports, and I have already made arrangements for you to be booked on the next flight to Amsterdam. My son and his wife live in the twin cities and they will join you tonight so that the girls have a female chaperone for their room and the boys will stay with my son and your chaperone. You know how to conduct yourselves and I look forward to seeing you in Europe! Does everyone understand the plan?"

And just like the ever popular bobbleheads that we see at sports stadiums all across America, these 6 young people, these 6 SMITS, shook their heads unanimously in agreement. And that was it.

Well, that was almost it. As the father of one of these 6 children, I cannot express to you the reader how difficult of a decision I now had to make. Because my daughter was not in my travel group, if I stayed behind with my daughter, that would mean that my travel group would have to continue on without me and, at least for a temporary amount of time, be redistributed to other existing travel groups. One of the things I really love about Mr. Horowitz is his ability to empower others-adults and students. He didn't tell me what to do, he didn't tell me what his preference would be...he simply said: "Of course, I will leave it up to you in terms of how you'd like to proceed with regards to staying behind or continuing on."

Thanks Mark! Do you ever have those times in your life where you wish someone would simply make a difficult decision for you?

I learned a lot about my "baby girl" on this 2008 trip to Denmark! I pulled her aside and I looked her in the eyes and I said something like: "Well, you've heard the plan. What do you think? I can stay back with you if you'd like. My travel group can be redistributed, that's not a problem".

There was no hesitation whatsoever on Abby's part and quite frankly her response did not surprise me in the least little bit. Without missing a beat and with the same direct eye contact I had just given her, my 10 year old, oldest child looked me in the eye and said: "No, dad, I am fine to stay here with my group." I believed her then, I believe her now and I know that she is a better, stronger young lady for having dealt with this adversity head on without her earthly daddy right at her side.

Abby, I am most proud of how you handled the situation and how it has impacted who you are today!

And so we hugged, said our goodbyes, knowing she would get her passport in the morning and my daughter went with her travel group and chaperone...and I rejoined the class, informing Mr. Horowitz of my decision, as we all began to somberly board the flight for Amsterdam.

I had just left my oldest child in Minneapolis with 5 of her peers, a student teacher, and 2 adults whom I did not know!

And this wasn't even the hard part!

Before boarding the flight to Amsterdam, I still needed to call home and inform my wife of the minor change in plans! Remember earlier when I said there are some times in life you just want someone else to make the decision for you? Well, I made the call and fortunately, or unfortunately depending on who's point of view you want to take, my wife did not answer her cell phone...so I left a message... as I boarded the international flight: "Hey, it's me and I just wanted to let you know that there has been a slight change of plans...Abby's chaperone left his and his travel group's passports in Milwaukee...the group can't retrieve them until tomorrow so she and her group are staying in Minneapolis at a hotel with him and Mr. Horowitz's son and daughter-in-law...I am going ahead to Europe with the rest of the group after having talked everything through with Abby...Abby and her group will come tomorrow...well, I just wanted to let you know that things have changed...I love you and will talk with you tomorrow..bye"

From what I recall, my wife didn't receive the message until approximately 10:00 p.m., Central Standard Time. By that time, Abby and company were watching Disney Channel, eating junk food and having a pillow fight somewhere in Minneapolis, Minnesota near the airport, I was somewhere over the eastern United States and my wife (I am sure of it) was somewhere between the state of "Are you kidding me?" and "Oh my God, what has my husband done!".

This book was published by me so clearly I lived to tell you the story. I have three other children who I hope will experience Room 23 and Denmark, and if "The case of the missing passports" happened to one of them, I would still make the same decision. I, like Mark Horowitz, believe in empowering young people and on that day in April, 2008, I saw my daughter grow up right before my very eyes. In a roundabout way, thank you Mr. Horowitz for being such an instrumental part of my daughter's life during that "crisis" that neither she, nor I (nor my wife!), will ever forget! As a teacher educator, I try to empower my students in the same way as Mark Horowitz has done for so many others throughout his brilliant career.

CHAPTER

THE RIPPLE EFFECT

At the university where I teach, we talk about the ripple effect. We have great commercials promoting how an education at our university is like a ripple effect. The commercial shows a drop of water that then ripples outward and goes on and on and on. When I think about Mark Horowitz and his impactful teaching, this is exactly what I think about. If Mark began teaching in 1969, and averaged roughly thirty students in his direct homeroom each year, one could safely say he has had a direct impact on nearly 1,200 students. I wish time would have allowed for me to introduce you to more of them, but suffice it to say he has certainly had a ripple effect in his teaching career on countless individuals, including this author.

MARK HOROWITZ'S IMPACT ON THE AUTHOR

Now that I am an aging father of four, I understand a little better the idea of living vicariously through one's children. Because

I knew my elementary school years at Golda Meir had been stellar, I knew from the day of her birth that I wanted my child to attend Golda Meir School. I wanted to live vicariously through Abby's years at the school that I loved. Being afforded the opportunity to chaperone the 2008 Denmark trip definitely allowed me to do so, but it actually began way before I had children of my own.

As mentioned earlier, my first real camping experience occurred as a result of being in Mr. Horowitz's class. Even though he was not traveling to Denmark in the 70's, there were numerous things I learned from him that I have taken with me into my teaching career.

One of the first things I did when I became a middle school teacher in Madison, Wisconsin was to become a certified ropes course facilitator. By doing so, this would afford my students the opportunity to get more out of their ropes course experience when we traveled there later in the school year. Each fall, my teaching partner and I would take our students to the school district forest for a three day experience that included camping, low ropes course and a high ropes course. I know that I would have never considered this type of learning as an option for students had it not been for my own fourth grade experiences in Room 23.

I know I am the educator I am today because of the direct influence Mark Horowitz has had on my life. There is no need to repeat all he has done for me to inspire me to become an educator, but let me tell you directly how he has influenced my teaching. As mentioned earlier, I believe one of the best ways to learn is through experiences. For some of our children, especially in urban communities, they come to school with limited experiences; some having never left their neighborhood or city. In twenty plus years of being an educator in Wisconsin and in the Milwaukee area, I am still amazed that we have young people who live in the city of Milwaukee, Wisconsin who do not know we live on a Great Lake. Going to their neighborhood school might be the extent of their lived experience.

When I became a middle school teacher in the Madison, Wisconsin Metropolitan School District, I vowed I would take with me my experiences as a student at Golda Meir School and try to expand the horizons of my students. I wish I could tell you I was as ingenious as Mark Horowitz and have traveled internationally with my students; nevertheless, one does what one can in creating his/her own persona. I am proud to tell you that during my seven years as a middle school teacher at both Cherokee Heights and Madison Middle School 2000, I have:

- Ridden the city bus with 20 middle school students and their 20 kindergarten buddies to the local farmer's market (I wish you could have seen the faces of all of the other passengers on that bus!).
- Spent an entire day with my wife and two bullied girls at Great America Amusement Park in Gurnee, Illinois, just because they asked me to take them!
- Arranged for a behind the scenes tours of the local NBC affiliate as a way of bringing language arts to life!
- Accompanied a student to Beloit College's Women and Girls in Science and Engineering Weekend Conference (one of my students was selected to attend; this was her first time away from home and her parents were unable to attend!)
- Arranged for students to attend the University of Wisconsin-Madison's Engineering Expo, whereby one of my sixth graders won first prize at a competition!
- Developed an integrated mathematics and language arts summer school program for middle school students with special needs and second language learners, including driving the students to and from school(frowned upon in regards to liability issues). This program featured a partnership with the Madison Police department as well.

- Personally driven(although much frowned upon as well) students from Madison, Wisconsin to summer school programs at the University of Wisconsin-Stout, approximately 4 hours away.

And then I grew restless! After seven years as a middle school educator, I received my first administrative position as principal of a small elementary school near Milwaukee, Wisconsin. Although I was no longer in direct contact with children in terms of a teaching responsibility, I was the "head learner" of a building and in doing so I was very supportive of teachers who wanted to extend the learning beyond the four walls of the classroom. While my stint as an elementary principal was a very short three years, during that time I had the privilege of supporting a third grade teacher's overnight trip to Point Beach State Forest near Manitowoc, Wisconsin and chaperoning three of my fourth grade classrooms to Camp Matawa in the beautiful Kettle Moraine Northern Unit of the State Forest. To this day, Camp Matawa remains a special place to me for learning as my own children regularly attend there, I recently completed two years on their board of directors and I continue to encourage anyone looking for an excellent outdoor learning experience for their students to choose Camp Matawa! In this era of accountability and state standards, it is very important that educators tie their work to standards. To those that say they don't have time to do the fun stuff like experiential learning because it takes away from test preparation and what students need to know for the test, I would offer that there is no better way to provide students with essential high order thinking skills than to have them experience life through cooperative adventures. It simply makes sense!

After ten years in K-12 education, I decided to pursue the teacher education side of education and have remained here as an Assistant Professor at Cardinal Stritch University. And yes, Mr. Mark Horowitz's influence still remains with me today. How else can you describe:

- flying in the descendant of a Holocaust survivor to present a powerful lesson on discrimination and bigotry for my college students;
- travelling with seven students and two colleagues to the Navajo Nation between fall and spring semesters for a week and half to understand Navajo culture and build relationships;
- using my sabbatical to make college access a viable option for white, rural elementary students who would be first-generation college students;
- helping to develop a once defunct urban middle school chess team and
- commiting to serve on the board of ImaginAction, Inc. which the reader will learn more about in the coming pages.

HIS IMPACT ON STUDENT TEACHERS

Mark Horowitz not only inspires his students through the Denmark trip, but his student teachers as well. During his 16 years of taking this trip, nearly 30 student teachers have also attended as chaperones, including a plethora from Cardinal Stritch University. If a trip of this magnitude can have a powerful impact on students, imagine the possibilities it has for a student teacher set to embark on his/her own teaching career. As mentioned earlier in the book, it is no accident that I plan a visit to Mr. Horowitz's classroom with my social studies methods students in the fall of every school year. Despite fall being the only time my course is offered at the undergraduate level (with the exception of an accelerated summer version), it serves as the perfect pipeline for potential student teachers. And eventual Denmark chaperones. To date, nearly a dozen student teachers from Cardinal Stritch University have had their student teaching experience with Mark Horowitz.

One of those student teachers who has certainly been affected by the ripple effect has been Lori-Cowen Briggs. I met Mrs. Briggs when she was an undergraduate student at our university enrolled in our teacher certification program. I will never forget Lori's first interaction at Golda Meir School. When I took her class to the annual visit to Mr. Horowitz's classroom, she had an important question at the end of his presentation that day: "Are there ever parents who change their minds or don't want to do this? Because I am a parent of a little girl and there is NO WAY I would let my child do this!" Yes, there are certainly parents who change their minds, and certainly parents need to know their children well enough to know whether or not this is for their family(see Appendix A). That is why every attempt is made on the front end to attract only families that really desire this experience.

I remember Lori being emphatic about not participating in a program like this as a parent. Then Lori was assigned to Mr. Horowitz's classroom for her student teaching placement and it is the expectation if one student teaches in this classroom, he or she also travels to Denmark with the class. And, as they say, the rest is history. My recollection is that Lori returned from Denmark transformed. "What an amazing teacher," I remember her recalling when I asked her about the experience. Upon returning stateside, Lori had nothing but positives to say about her experiences overseas. The future teacher, who had been so adamant against her own child participating in a program like this, was now seeking my advice as to whether or not to pull her own child from their local suburban school district and apply to attend Golda Meir School. My response was simply, if it were my child, I would do so. Due to various family circumstances, Lori was unable to do so for her daughter. At least for now, Lori's daughter would have to experience Golda Meir School vicariously through conversations with her mom about her student teaching experience.

During the 1999-2000 school year, Rebecca Haushatter did her student teaching with Mark Horowitz. "He was an extraordinary person to learn from," says Rebecca. "I was incredibly fortunate to have my student teaching experience with him and to be a part of the trip to Denmark-a great teaching and learning experience."

"One of the first things that really struck me the most about Mark and Golda Meir School in general was this (what I would consider) unique phenomenon of so many children choosing to stay inside during lunch recess!", said Rebecca. I believe it is safe to say that in a number of schools across America, the circumstances that lead to one staying in for recess usually revolve around misbehavior. To the contrary at Golda Meir!

Students can choose from a number of activities to attend every day during lunch recess, from gospel choir, to intramural sports to simply staying in and talking with friends. Rebecca said "I remember spending lunch in the classroom helping students with questions and homework or just having a nice meal with them." Even my own daughter, now three years removed from Mr. Horowitz's classroom, still chooses to spend some of her lunch time with middle school friends visiting her old teacher's classroom. Talk about an open door policy...

As an educator, I can imagine what this trip does for a future teacher because it allows him/her to see the great potential that exists to make learning fun, relevant and meaningful. Says Rebecca: "On the trip, the students were very excited and a little afraid. They were as well prepared as they could be for what was ahead. I remember the anticipation on the flight over and the excitement as we landed. The kids seemed to have the most fun at school with their Danish counterparts...and at Legoland! They shared great stories on the flight home and for weeks after until summer arrived."

As I said earlier, not everything that is tested matters...and everything that matters is usually not tested.

"Mark Horowitz helped me learn to take advantage of the opportunities life gives you and never look back," says Rebecca. This is a priceless lesson regardless of whether or not one is training to become a teacher.

Rebecca goes on to say the following: "While I was student teaching in Mr. Horowitz's classroom, I was accepted into the Peace Corps. The trip to Denmark was my first visit overseas, and I think it really opened me up to traveling and exploring other cultures. I was certainly more comfortable in unfamiliar situations after the Denmark trip. I left that summer to teach English as a Peace Corps volunteer in a rural Jordanian village. The latter experience was one of the most meaningful and rewarding times of my life. Since then, I have traveled to Thailand, Peru, Egypt, France, Italy, Australia and many other places. Denmark was just the beginning of many travel adventures for me."

Denmark was just the beginning...

"When I returned from the Peace Corps, I did not pursue a career in teaching, but was awarded a graduate fellowship to study public service. After graduating, I began working for a small nonprofit focusing on meeting community needs through volunteerism. The nonprofit sector is where I plan to stay for now, but I know that many of the skills I learned as a teacher in Mr. Horowitz's classroom have translated well to the nonprofit arena."

SHARING THE SIDEWALK

In spring, 2005, Mr. Scott Middlestadt had the opportunity to learn from Mark Horowitz as a student teacher who would travel to Denmark. "The trip changed my outlook on life," says Scott. 'It opened my eyes to a lot of things and showed me that the rest of the world doesn't share our American vision on many things!" Now a fourth grade teacher at a suburban parochial school near Milwaukee, Mr. Middlestadt spoke of his Danish experience and time with Mr. Horowitz as if it were just the other day.

"Mark Horowitz is one of the few teachers I have met who regretted the end of the school year. He has got to be the most driven person I have ever met. He has the right personality to pull off something of this magnitude!" Scott believes Mr. Horowitz could have done anything he wanted in life, but Scott is glad that Mark chose to become a teacher because Scott has learned quite a bit from the Denmark experience and Mr. Horowitz. "Any chance I get," said Scott, "I talk about my experience in Copenhagen. The atmosphere in that city was so peaceful. As a result of that trip, I now teach a world travel unit where by students choose any country they are interested in learning about and they research the country in depth across various curricular areas. They spend a month studying the culture, planning an itinerary, and putting together a budget that would support a trip to the country.

The Denmark experience also impacted my world view. It taught me that it is ok to be happy with what you have, to not necessarily want bigger and better. I am comfortable with the home I have and the life I have provided for my wife and daughter. My Danish host, Dorta, did not own a car and she biked everywhere. She even gave me a bike to use when I was there and those daily bicycle rides gave me a different perspective on life".

Beyond Scott's initial visit with Mr. Horowitz's group in 2005, Scott has continued to travel to Denmark vicariously through his wife and daughter who visited Denmark a few years after him. They, of course, stayed with Dorta! A hotel would simply not do justice to the authenticity of the trip! Scott's daughter went to school in Denmark while she was there and for three weeks in the summer, A Danish student came to America to stay with the Middlestadts.

Does Mark Horowitz really and truly know and understand how far reaching his program is?

And just like the pages of a good book make the reader want to turn the page to the next chapter, these follow up Danish connections did the same for Scott. He said that the subsequent spin offs from his initial visit to Denmark made him want to explore his Scandinavian heritage more in depth. He started to talk about this with his mother and when his wife and daughter travelled to Denmark, they eventually made their way to Norway and found a farm that had been in their family's heritage for years.

And to think that a Milwaukee Public Schools teacher had something to do with that great moment!

I would have to say that of all of my interviewees for this book, Scott Middlestadt proved to be the most heart-warming! Maybe I am biased because he is one of the few men who have chosen elementary education as a career. Maybe my bias stems from the fact that he is a former student of mine and a graduate of the Cardinal Stritch University MAT (Master's of Art in Teaching) program. Or maybe I was simply impressed by being able to see and hear Mark Horowitz's direct influence on Scott's fifth grade classroom! "Whatever Mark Horowitz does, he does it all the way! Even on the camping trips he provided for his students, he really expects the kids to do everything! They can and they do! As a chaperone, whether it was the Denmark trip or any other field trip, I was just there to make sure kids were safe and following through on the expectations".

As a direct result of being a student teacher with Mr. Horowitz, Scott now incorporates neighborhood walks into his daily routine and schedule. "I saw the benefits of learning how to travel together safely in a group from our trip to Denmark. It really is a great experience to travel together as a group. I am teaching them how to read the environment around them. This is something that many young students don't do naturally, so it is an art that must be taught. Once they become aware, it changes the dynamics of the class. When we leave for our walks, I ask my students 'Look around you...what do you see?'

It's a simple, yet powerful request, one that is sure to open up the hearts and minds of anyone who takes the time to do this. According to Scott, the kids "start to appreciate having a conversation because they are walking and talking with a purpose. Some parents have told me that it has been the high point of the day for their children." Let me see if I understand this correctly:

Fifth graders would rate a walk in their school's neighborhood with their teacher as the high point of their day versus lunch or recess on the playground?

"It's different than being on the playground," says Scott. "You have to learn to respect your neighbors' property. We pick up litter if we see it. When an adult is approaching us, I make sure that we are respectful and move over to the side. It's important to me that my students learn to share the sidewalk with others". Knowing what I know about Mr. Middlestadt, I am quite sure he and his class continue the learning once they return to the class by debriefing the walk and making curricular connections.

When thinking about this simple experience of taking a neighborhood walk, the proverbial question comes to mind: "If a tree falls in a forest and no one is there to see it, does it make a sound?" So I pose the following to the reader: If Mr. Middlestadt and his fifth grade class go for their daily walk and they only have conversations among themselves, have they impacted anyone else's life?

I have had many wise guides in my life so I am unsure as to which one of them actually told me this, but it has stayed with me into adulthood: be careful of your actions and words because someone is always watching you. I have found that piece of advice to be so true and I believe Mr. Middlestadt would say the same because one day his principal approached him and said a gift had arrived for Mr. Middlestadt's class. The principal went on to explain that a neighbor had taken the time to email the principal and inquire about the male teacher who takes his kids on a walk every day. The neighbor commented on how thoughtful the children are, how mannerly they conduct themselves and that "they seem so happy!" The neighbor was so moved by this daily occurrence (one has to wonder if this might have been the high point of the day for the neighbor?) that he wanted to do something for the teacher and his students. The gift waiting in the office was a check for $300 to be used exclusively for any other fieldtrips Mr. Middlestadt's students might want to attend that might require more than a neighborhood walk!

I know Scott Middlestadt did not set out on these daily walks with the intention of earning money. However, does the reader see what happens when you "share the sidewalk" with others? I guess you could say that this neighbor had just indirectly met Mark Horowitz!

Says Scott: "Mark Horowitz is one in a million. I do not know that anyone else could do this Denmark trip the way that he does. I mean, I am sure others could physically do the trip with students, but it wouldn't have the same impact. I think about myself trying to attempt a trip of that magnitude! And I just don't see it happening. But then again, I have only been teaching six years and Mr. Horowitz has been teaching over forty years!" Don't sell yourself short Scott. You have got plenty of time to make a difference in the lives of many children. In fact, you are already doing so by taking your students on a daily walk. The journey of a thousand miles begins with one step.

SIX DEGREES OF SEPARATION: RAFE ESQUITH

Readers who follow the field of education may now be asking themselves: 'Mark Horowitz knows Rafe Esquith?,' the author of such popular books as *Teach Like Your Hair's on Fire* and *There are No Shortcuts?* Was Rafe a student of Mr. Horowitz at some point in time? Or vice versa? Did Rafe go to Denmark?

The answer to these questions is "no", although I cannot say for certain whether Rafe Esquith has ever been to Denmark at some point in his life! He very well may have. I decided to talk about Rafe Esquith in this final chapter simply because teachers like Esquith(or Ron Clark or Erin Gruwell for that matter) are few and far between. For the reader who may not be familiar with Mr. Esquith, I wanted to share a little bit about this fabulous educator who certainly belongs in the same category as Mark Horowitz!

In Thernstrom and Thernstrom's 2003 book *No Excuses: Closing the Racial Gap in Learning,* the authors bring to life this dynamic teacher of Hobart Elementary School in Los Angeles, California. The Hobart School where Rafe Esquith teaches runs from 7:58 a.m. to 2:58 p.m., but Esquith opens his classroom doors at 6:30 a.m. every morning, and most students are working by 7:00 a.m.! (As an aside, my son was home ill from school recently. At the time of this writing, he was 100 days from his Danish departure. Later, that evening, my son literally begged me to let him go back to school tomorrow because he had a computer program to finish for Mr. Horowitz. My son was at school by 7:00 a.m. the next morning!)

According to Thernstrom and Thernstrom (2003), Esquith also has a program of after school activities that keep the students who want to stay until 6:00 p.m. (as an aside: Mark Horowitz spends one night a week after school coaching a girls soccer team in the gymnasium at Golda Meir School). Rafe Esquith gives guitar lessons at recess and lunchtime for those who wish to remain in the room. (Mark Horowitz is also the director of the Golda Meir Chamber Ensemble, a group of students who want more music and practice in his room during their lunchtime!)

Saturday mornings Rafe Esquith works with some of his former students in grades 6-10 on Algebra, Shakespeare and SAT preparation. Saturday afternoons, its back to music. During the sixteen weeks of school vacation, his students continue to come to class, although their regular classroom is occupied by another class-one of the costs of Los Angele's staggered school year. Esquith meets them in the auditorium, in the library, or on benches outside if necessary. He also takes them on trips (funded by donations) to Washington D.C., South Dakota and elsewhere.

In addition to these longer trips, Esquith takes his kids to concerts, ball games and restaurants. Before they go, they learn to sit quietly at the concert, and to clap at the right time. Their presence at a restaurant never disturbs the other patrons; they talk quietly. (Mark Horowitz's students study regions from each of the seven continents, often times culminating in a culinary visit to a local restaurant; not to mention an American prepared Danish luncheon held at Golda Meir School one week prior to departing for Denmark).

I used MapQuest and found that Golda Meir School, in Milwaukee, Wisconsin is 2,117 miles from Hobart Elementary School in Los Angeles, California. Rafe Esquith and Mark Horowitz, however, are only six degrees of separation from one another in terms of their "holistic approach to educating children!" (Janet Carr, Personal Communications, 2011).

At the time of this book being written, Megan Harper and Jill Opie had yet to secure their own classrooms; due in large part to the fact that they were completing their student teaching with Mark Horowitz in the fall of 2010 and spring of 2011, respectively and they plan to attend as chaperones for the 2011 trip. In a joint interview, they spoke at length about what their time under Mark's tutelage has meant to them.

"There wasn't a day that went by in student teaching where he didn't talk about the trip," said Jill. "His sense of goal and mission is amazing. I love that the Denmark trip was the focal point of the school year for the students. I could see myself doing something like this for my students."

Said Meghan: "I don't know that I would do a trip with students, but I love the idea of having a focal point or topic for the year and having all of the subject areas connect to it. I loved how he connected with so many different teachers in the building. People are so devoted to him... art, music and people like Dick Marks who came in to our classroom to do teambuilding exercises with the kids! I saw immediately the impact this had on the class community and I would love to do these types of things in my classroom."

Meghan and Jill were the envy of their student teaching seminars. No other student teachers were planning to go on a two week European field trip with their students. I also suspect very few of their peers were thrown into the responsibilities of student teaching as they were. "When I began student teaching at Golda Meir, I had to attend a meeting for all of the student teachers in the building. Mr. Hanley (Golda Meir principal) and Mr. Becker (Dean of Students) asked us 'What mid-day option would you like to offer?' It was an expectation of student teachers" said Meghan.

"After being there only a couple of days, Mark had me teaching social studies and it was great", said Jill. "He allowed me to incorporate technology into my lessons and he was always very complimentary towards my efforts! When I was teaching about slavery and the Holocaust, he would add at the end 'These were some of the worst human atrocities our world has ever seen...because people didn't respect cultural differences...and that is why we are taking this trip to Denmark..."

Besides the content, there were so many other things Meghan and Jill learned from Mr. Horowitz; things that certainly can't be measured by a standardized test nor are they taught in university methods courses. "Mark was constantly teaching them to be aware of their surroundings", said Jill. "Every now and then, he would make changes within our room and then he would ask the students 'Does anybody notice anything different in the room?'...and it could be something as small as a miniature Van Gogh painting, and then he would launch into a lesson on that painting. It was amazing."

"He taught the kids how to shake hands. We had a high school student come to our classroom on a weekly basis to volunteer his time. On his first day, all thirty kids went up to the young man and introduced themselves, giving him a firm handshake. Mark taught them the value of a good handshake". Jill continued: "He also taught them how to be reflective and thankful. I never thought about sending or taking a gift to my host family, but Mark has fully prepared the students for all of this."

DREAMS + ACTION=IMAGINACTION!

I'll never forget the day Pete Wilson walked into my office on the Cardinal Stritch University campus. At the time, Pete was a graduate student in our MAT program for second career educators. Pete was one of many graduate students who had chosen to return to school after having had a different career other than educator. "Corey, I just don't know.....I don't know if I have made the right decision or not regarding going into education. I don't see very many men in the field". He was right. There aren't many of us. But there is a Mark Horowitz and Pete's timing was right on.

One of my favorite classes to teach at our university is the Social Studies Methods course. I love social studies because it is really the study of us, human beings, over time, and the many similarities and differences that often separate us and sometimes unite us. To water down such a fascinating field by having students memorize dates and regurgitate facts is mind boggling to me. I won't do it to children and I try to impress upon my pre-service teachers the importance of making social studies come alive for students. So every semester as a part of my undergraduate course (unfortunately the graduate students do not have this option because their course meets during the evenings), I take my students to Golda Meir School to meet Mr. Horowitz and his SMITS. At the time when Pete Wilson came to my office, we were on the verge of making the annual pilgrimage to Golda Meir, and so I invited Pete to join us. I am glad he did. I know he is too!

Prior to 2011, Golda Meir School did not have an elevator on site. Thus, for those on crutches like Pete Wilson, who had recently sustained an injury requiring his use of them, the stairs were unforgiving; nevertheless, he ascended them and made his way to Room 23, the same Room 23 that I had called home in the 1978-1979 school year, to join me and my undergraduate class for the presentation by Mark Horowitz. Because I do not tell my students why we are going to Golda Meir School for the visit, it is always fascinating for me to watch my students' reactions when these SMITS and their fabulous teacher begin speaking in Danish and then proceed to tell us about this fifteen day "field trip" on which they embark! If I am not mistaken, I do not think I revealed to Pete why we were going to Golda Meir School. I believe I simply said: "I have a male teacher I think you should meet".

At the end of the presentation by Mark Horowitz and SMITS, my students were amazed. I think Pete was too! I remember Pete getting up on his crutches and walking over to shake Mr. Horowitz's hand and saying something like: "Wow! How can I get the chance to student teach in your classroom?"

Pete traveled with the class in 2004 and enjoyed it just as much, if not more, than the students (I had the same experience when I was able to attend as a chaperone in 2008). Pete Wilson has always had a love of photography and traveling. Therefore, it comes as no surprise that upon completing our MAT program, Pete became a multiage elementary teacher at Racine Montessori School (RMS) in Racine, Wisconsin, a city of 50,000 residents approximately 30 miles south of Milwaukee. Pete's class consisted of fourth, fifth and sixth graders, team taught by Pete and another teacher. Unfortunately (or fortunately, depending upon how one looks at it), Pete's teaching partner was not fond of experiential learning opportunities. One day she said to him: "I don't really want to do any excursions outside of school, so feel free to create the things you'd like to and I will stay behind with the other kids". So he did!

While his teaching partner stayed behind with the fourth and sixth graders, Mr. Wilson arranged for a long weekend fieldtrip to Springfield, Illinois, the land of Lincoln, to study about our sixteenth president of the United States of America.

Springfield, Illinois is about five hours south of Racine, Wisconsin. The students stayed in a hotel and visited the Lincoln Museum and other Lincoln-related attractions. I do not know about you, but the extent of my learning about Abraham Lincoln was a *filmstrip* (readers born after 1990 probably have no frame of reference!), plus the blurb in my history textbook and a worksheet undoubtedly!

While his teaching partner stayed behind with the fifth and sixth graders, Mr. Wilson ventured north about three hours to a tiny town called Manitowoc, Wisconsin. Part of the Wisconsin Fourth Grade Social Studies Curriculum calls for the study of the state. While the majority of Wisconsin fourth grade teachers focus on the State capitol of Madison, Wisconsin (and often include a trip to the beautiful domed building), Mr. Wilson went a little further beyond the typical textbook. In Manitowoc, Wisconsin resides the Wisconsin Maritime Museum, detailing Wisconsin's maritime history. Undoubtedly the highlight of this museum is the opportunity to spend the night on board the USS Cobra, a real maritime submarine! My understanding is that this experience is not for those who might be claustrophobic! Pete recalled one day the story of one of his students who had trouble just spending the night at a friend's house in Racine. Can you even begin to imagine the fears that student might have stepping aboard a US submarine, knowing she would be spending the night there? She overcame her fear, and learned quite a bit in the process! Thanks in large part to her very caring teacher.

Anyone who ventures outside the four walls of his or her classroom with students on extended learning opportunities such as these has to be a caring individual! While I know that this type of learning does not bode well for all educators, I do believe that we would see better student engagement and an increase in student achievement if more of these opportunities existed for students. I believe this is especially true for those students for whom these types of travels are either limited or non-existent.

Imaginaction, Inc. was born with the sixth graders in Mr. Wilson's class at RMS; however, at the time this was not known to Mr. Wilson. While his teaching partner stayed behind with the fourth and fifth graders, Mr. Wilson headed west with the sixth graders to the Pacific Northwest and Canada. The unique thing about this fieldtrip is that the students played an even bigger part in the planning and preparation of the trip. The students made phone calls, did research and helped organize a plethora of fundraising opportunities. Pete combined his love of national parks and travel and learning by taking the students on a five day, four night excursion that included stops at Olympic National Park, the Hoh Rainforest, the town of Forks (setting of the hit movie and book Twilight) and a ferry ride to British Columbia for a day of learning. As a social studies methods professor, it is a no-brainer as to how a trip like this could easily be connected to state social studies standards and the teaching of political science, behavioral science, geography, economics and history. It simply makes sense!

"If you imagine yourself going somewhere or doing something, that's fine, but I really do believe that in order for what you imagine to actually take place, you have to take action!" Thus the origin of Pete Wilson's new non-profit entity: Imaginaction. Pete decided to leave RMS in search of teaching opportunities in the Milwaukee area; truly believing that his fresh approach to teaching through experiential learning would land him a perfect spot at the very place where he had experienced it himself as a student teacher. At the end of the 2009-2010 school year, Pete Wilson, along with some four hundred other educators, found himself a "casualty of bureaucracy" (my words for what took place) and out of a teaching position at Golda Meir School, where he had been the Math Teacher Leader (MTL) for two years. Having left the Milwaukee Public School system, Mr. Wilson began brainstorming how he could still "have his cake and eat it too" (my words, not his!). In the summer of 2010, he began the process of creating a non-profit organization which he aptly titled "Imaginaction". For more information on Imaginaction, I strongly encourage readers to check us out at: *https://sites.google.com/site/imaginactionwi/*

I say us because I am proud to tell the reader I sit on the board of directors for Imaginaction and I plan to remain there as long as Pete needs me. I have seen this grow from one man's vision to an entity that will have a direct impact on countless lives of young people. Sounds very familiar doesn't it?

In summer of 2011, Imaginaction will launch for the first time with its inaugural group of students. The plan is for Mr. Wilson and his group of teachers to spend four weeks in the summer teaching fifth graders about the Pacific Northwest through grass roots, integrated curriculum. At the end of the four week summer school session, the group will head west, just like Pete Wilson did back at RMS, to the Pacific Northwest. For many of the students, if not all of them, this will be their first time on an airplane.

During the summer of 2009, I had the opportunity to travel with Mr. Wilson to the Pacific Northwest to see the various sites he had visited in the past with students from RMS. It was a fabulous experience, and I could see how this trip had the potential to grow exponentially. By the time we were done with our trip, Pete had added several new stops, or should I say learning experiences, to what I would consider an already excellent learning experience for students. Not only will the 2011 "Imaginaction Pioneers" (my words) experience the original destinations, minus the Canadian experience, they will also visit the Makah Indian Reservation, U.S. Coast Guard facility and the Fero Marine life Center. Last time I checked, most American students only accessed these places by simply reading about them in their social studies text books.

THE HEIR APPARENT?

Probably the toughest words I have yet to print are the ones that follow: Mark Horowitz won't teach forever. Despite that fact, will the Denmark trip cease to exist as well? I suppose with a change in administration, budget cuts and retirement, it is a very real possibility and that would be a tragic loss to the city of Milwaukee and future Golda Meir students. That is, of course, unless one can find someone who can carry the baton, who can run the good race, fight the good fight...someone who knows this program intimately like his or her own heart. Someone, perhaps like Karen Backes Felder, who sits in a unique position as someone who does know the Denmark program like the back of her hand.

"I feel extremely fortunate to have traveled to Denmark 3 times as part of this program", said Karen. "My first trip was as a 4th grader. On this trip, I met my host, who has become a close, lifelong friend. We did not go to Legoland or spend the night in Amsterdam on this trip. It was only the second year of the program and Mark was still working to develop it. My second trip to Denmark was as a 7th grade junior chaperone. At the time, Golda Meir did not have middle school classes (the school now encompasses a full 6th through 8th grade). I was a student at Roosevelt Middle School of the Arts. My mom worked hard to help my teachers understand the value of the trip, even though I had to miss school for it. On this trip, I remember that our trip to the Anne Frank House had a much stronger impact on me. I read *The Diary of Anne Frank* before I traveled the second time. My third trip to Denmark came when I was a student teacher in Mark's classroom.

It was incredible for me to experience this trip from three different perspectives. As a 4th grader it was a great learning experience that I worked hard to prepare for during the school year. As a 7th grader, it was more of a fun chance to visit my host and her family again, as well as an opportunity to assist with the traveling. It was also a great educational opportunity, but I did not spend time in school preparing for the trip. My Danish was beyond rusty by this point, and I experienced more homesickness on this trip than I did as a 4th grader. Firstly, email was more accessible and I received daily emails from my parents, which served as a constant reminder of what I was "missing" back home. It was easier not to be homesick when I had less contact with my family. I missed them, but it was easier to let myself become absorbed in what I was doing on the trip rather than thinking about the things I might be missing out on at home.

Secondly, I think I was less prepared for the trip in some ways because I wasn't in Mark's class getting ready every day the way I had been as a 4th grader. The trip is what ties together everything that happens in that classroom. Finally, as a 4th grader, almost my entire class was there with me, so I had the support of many friends who were experiencing the same things I was. I didn't have this peer support when I traveled as a 7th grader. Mark now brings a small group of junior counselors on most trips, so they are probably able to rely on each other some.

My third trip as a student teacher was an unbelievable experience. I student taught in Mark's class in the fall of the 2008-09 school year. I loved being in the classroom from the beginning of the school year. I was able to see how Mark begins the year with high expectations. The fact that the students in Mark's classes get along with one another so well is no accident. He works hard to teach them to work together and appreciate one another. I was also fortunate to see how much the students grew and matured over the school year because I was with them at the very beginning. (I met them at the first Denmark Trip meeting the previous school year.) I decided to make the trip, even though I was no longer student teaching in Mark's class at the time. In fact, I was living in Ames, Iowa with my fiancé, about to get married. We returned in mid-May and I got married May 24th!!

Looking back, this was an extremely busy time in my life, but I'm so glad I decided to go on the trip. I stayed with a new family this time, but I was able to spend time with my previous host. Even though we hadn't seen each other for nearly 10 years, it was like no time had passed- our friendship was as strong as ever. I had much more responsibility on this trip than I did on either of my two previous trips. I will admit that I was a bit nervous about being responsible for students so far away from home. However, the class is so well prepared for the trip by the time they travel that chaperoning them is not as challenging as it could be.

I believe I am the only person to have traveled with Mark and his students in all 3 of these roles. I feel so fortunate to have been able to travel all three times. I recently finished my first year of teaching. I work as a gifted and talented resource teacher in a small Wisconsin school district. Part of the reason I was able to obtain my current teaching position in such a difficult teaching job market was my experience working with Mark at Golda Meir. I had so many valuable experiences on all three of my trips. I am also a proud new mother and I am looking forward to taking my husband and son to Denmark someday to meet my host. My husband loves the idea because I have talked so much about Denmark and how much I enjoyed myself there. We are just waiting for our son to be old enough to appreciate the trip, and to save up enough money for all of us to travel!

These trips to Denmark have helped me develop a great love for traveling and experiencing life and cultures in different places. I have also been to Germany, Italy, and the Bahamas with school organized groups. I think I got more out of these trips because of my previous experiences traveling with Mark Horowitz. I learned to be flexible when traveling. Seeing this trip from 3 different perspectives helped me understand the educational value of traveling to a different place to experience new things and strengthened my desire to be a teacher.

I am now an elementary school teacher and one of the big reasons I wanted to become a teacher was because of Mark's influence. He helped me see how exciting it can be to be a part of a class where hard work is expected and great things can be accomplished. Mark helped shape my career path and I love my profession dearly and am proud of what I have chosen to spend my life doing. Mark taught me that 4th graders can do just about anything, except keep their desks arranged where they are supposed to be! (This is something he actually said to me when I was student teaching in his class. You can tell that he really believes it and I think he is right!)

My ultimate goal is to one day take over the Denmark program! Mark will have to retire eventually..."

Should Karen Backes Felder be fortunate to land a teaching job in the Milwaukee Public Schools system, I think I know of a school that might want to pursue her...

HOW THIS BOOK CAME ABOUT

July 9, 2009. The genesis for this book: Lakefront Brewery, Milwaukee, Wisconsin. Two tables full of adults and children; mostly American, but 1 Danish family-my host family-and host to numerous other Americans throughout this great international experience. A Milwaukee fish fry. A very loud polka band. Laughter and fond memories of what has been...and what is yet to come.

When interviewing the many people associated with Mark Horowitz and the Denmark experience for this book, I was struck by my conversation with Mrs. Janet Carr. Appendices C and D are compliments of Janet's contributions to this work. They consist of a sample fundraising letter, a personal reflection on the trip and a request for a mayoral proclamation. In addition to these contributions and the many words shared in our conversation, I felt compelled to end this book with a "grook"('gruk' in Danish) she shared with me. She indicated, for her, it summed up her feelings about Mark Horowitz. A "grook" is a form of short aphoristic poem. It was invented by the Danish poet and scientist Piet Hein. He wrote over 7,000 of them, most in Danish or English, published in 20 volumes. Some say that the name is short for "Grin & sUK" ("laugh & sigh" in Danish), but Piet Hein said he felt that the word had come out of thin air.

WHAT'S NEXT?

We none of us know
What Man's future will bring:
But his previous
History shows
That he's clever enough
To do any damn thing
That he's foolish enough
to propose.

-Piet Hein

I believe the words of my son's Danish parents, Torben and Charlotte, also provide a fitting end to this work. "Mr. Horowitz is very passionate about the program, and takes pride in delivering a professional experience for both the students and their parents. This is not just another exchange program, but a program that educates and matures the students. Despite the differences in age, Mr. Horowitz is also a very important and strong role model to the teachers that are part of the program. It is hard to see who would be able to take over from him but we certainly hope that the program will continue to the benefit of both the US and the Danish students".

Thank you, Mr. Mark Horowitz. Or as they say in the happiest country in the world (Legatum Institute, 2010):

TAK.
TUSINTAK.
MANGETAK.

ABOUT

GOLDA MEIR SCHOOL

(Taken from the school's official website)

Golda Meir School 's Gifted and Talented Program was implemented in the early 1970s as part of Milwaukee 's magnet school program. On May 4, 1979, Golda Meir School, originally known as 4th Street School, was renamed and re-dedicated in honor of Golda Meir, the former Prime Minister of Israel, who attended the school from 1906-1909.

Although Golda Meir School follows the traditional MPS curriculum, the teachers and staff broaden and extend the curriculum by providing real-world learning opportunities for their students. The school's close proximity to downtown Milwaukee provides a community classroom where students have easy access to key landmarks, cultural centers and educational organizations, such as:

- The Milwaukee Art Museum
- The Milwaukee Public Museum

- The Jewish Museum
- Summerfest
- Manpower International
- A variety of ethnic restaurants
- First Stage Children's Theater
- Milwaukee Youth Symphony Orchestra
- Milwaukee County Historical Society, including Father Pere Marquette's landing spot and park

Golda Meir School provides a challenging curriculum for a diverse student body from Milwaukee and the surrounding suburbs in grades 3-8.

GOLDA MEIR'S ADMINISTRATIVE LEADERSHIP:

From Past to Present

My mother, in her opening comments, has already touched upon one of the leaders of Golda Meir School, my elementary principal, Mr. Albin Kaczmarek. In putting this work together, I had the utmost pleasure of dining with the past and present (Mr. Tom Hanley) leadership of Golda Meir School. In fact these two men represent the only administrators Golda Meir School has ever known since its inception as a school for the Gifted and Talented. At the end of the 2010-2011 school year, Mr. Hanley will retire from MPS, leaving very big shoes to fill for the third Golda Meir principal! Having been an elementary principal at one time in my career, I have wanted to know what it would be like to be the "Head Learner" of a dynamic place like Golda Meir School.

"We don't get a lot of applications to fill the position of the Golda Meir Principalship," says Mr. Hanley. "There is a perception that it (the Golda Meir principalship) is too much work, too difficult and too high profile of a position." "However," added Mr. Kaczmarek, "the environment the principal creates is so important. Because Golda has such a diversified teaching force, you automatically draw parents to the building."

Having been both a student and a parent at Golda Meir, I have always wondered how the educational leader of the building "gets away with" teachers taking students out of the building for so many learning opportunities: Madison, Wisconsin, New York, NY, Virginia and Denmark. The list goes on. Apparently, the key is to ask the right questions. "You can't ask the wrong question," says Mr. Kaczmarek, "when working within a large bureaucracy." It has become clear to me that an effective Golda Meir principal is one who,according to Mr. Kaczmarek, "allows the teachers to do these great things for kids... allows them to pursue their interests and passions."

"We try to make the most out of all the adults in our building," said Mr. Hanley. "For example, when student teachers come into our building, we include them in every staff meeting; we devote a bulletin board to introducing them to the Golda community, and we ask them what special gift or talent they would like to share with our students during our noon options program."

"Mark really wanted to do this (take students to Denmark). So, when he came to me to pitch his idea, I said 'How can I help?'" And the rest they say is history!

Prior to becoming Golda Meir's second principal, Mr. Hanley, was a fifth grade teacher at Golda Meir. During his time as a fifth grade teacher there, he too would venture internationally with students-to France. "I thought he was nuts," said Tom Hanley during our lunch interview, referring to Mr. Horowitz's Denmark trip. "However, when I received students from his class for my fifth grade class the next year, I noticed his students had the ability to organize and be self-reliant."

Reflecting on his years as the first principal of Golda Meir School, Mr. Kaczmarek talked about the importance of merchandising. The concept of speciality schools in MPS was a new idea, and so having students travel internationally could add to an already well-established reputation. "We had to get enough positive publicity to our school," said Mr. Kaczmarek. "The Denmark program was good for those students who got in to Mr. Horowitz's class."

"The experience proves to kids that they can do anything!"

APPENDIX

At the beginning of May of each school year, the following letter is distributed to all 90 third grade students at Golda Meir School, many of whom are interested in obtaining one of the coveted 30 spots in Mr. Horowitz's fourth grade classroom.

Mr. Horowitz pens this letter on the return plane ride to the United States, while 30 some American students are either fast asleep or busy reminiscing about the past 15 days abroad!

RE: Mr. Horowitz's 4th Grade Danish Study & travel Experience Opportunity

Dear Parents/Guardians of Third Graders:

As many of you already know, I have traveled to Denmark with my fourth grade classes in each of the last sixteen years. The trips have been among the most rewarding experiences in my 42 years of teaching. They have been experiences that my students will remember for the rest of their lives. Our hosts at Dyssegardsskolen have also had favorable reactions to the trips. The parents of many of this year's third graders have already expressed an interest in serving as hosts for our fourth graders next year. The following information is offered to help you decide whether you would like your child to be considered for participation in the Denmark 2011 program.

We expect all of the children in my class to travel with us. Much of our classroom curriculum is designed to prepare the students for the trip. This includes studying Danish culture, learning to speak Danish, studying the metric system, learning about international travel and communications, and reading Danish literature. We also study about the lives of Vincent Van Gogh and Anne Frank, and we visit the Van Gogh Museum and the Anne Frank House during our 2 days in Amsterdam on our return trip home from Denmark.

The trip, itself, is designed to help the children learn about a culture different from ours, and in doing so, to learn more about our own culture and values. Each child will live for two weeks with a Danish child and his/her family. Children will attend school with their hosts and participate in afterschool activities with them. They may do some traveling with host families on weekends. We will probably also take three trips together: a walking trip through the center of Copenhagen, an excursion to the city of Roskilde, about 25 miles from Copenhagen, to see the Viking Ship Museum and the Roskilde Cathedral, burial site of Danish Kings and Queens of the last 500 years, and a trip to Legoland, an amusement park.

The family of each child participating in the Denmark program will be expected to participate in a number of activities, including attending each parents' meeting. We expect to have meetings in June, September, January and March. Each family will have the opportunity to participate in our fund-raising acgtivities, which will begin during the summer. (the cost of the 2009-2010 trip was $1,550 per student and included airfare, insurance, expenses in Copenhagen, and a 24-hour stay in Amsterdam on the way home. This did not include spending money, passports and gifts for the host families.) Each family will be expected to follow the schedule that they will be given in the fall for making payments for the trip. Travel dates are tentatively scheduled for late April/early May.

As you and your child consider this unique educational opportunity, please remember that it is also a demanding personal challenge. It would be important that each child be able and willing to conduct himself/herself in an exemplary manner during the trip. Parents and children should understand that if a child demonstrates during the school year that he/she would be unable to behave in an appropriate manner during the trip, then he/she may not be invited to travel with us. We would try to refund all of the money that had been paid. However, the airfare, once paid to our travel agent, is not refundable.

To help you decide whether you would like your child considered for placement in my fourth grade room, you may be interested in some of the other areas of our curriculum, which include the following:

Reading: Our program is literature-based. The children read award-winning novels rather than a basal reader.

Mathematics: We will be using Everyday Mathematics, the school adopted mathematics curriculum, and a variety of other math materials. There will be an emphasis on problem solving as well as basic facts and computation.

Social Studies: We will study cultures from all around the world in addition to Denmark.

Spelling: I have prepared a challenging spelling curriculum.

Computer: The children will use Apple IIe computers to develop keyboarding skills and to learn to write programs. They will use Macintosh computers to learn to use a word processing program, to use curriculum-related software, to access the Internet, and to send and receive e-mail.

If you have questions that I haven't answered regarding this opportunity, please don't hesitate to contact me. I am looking forward to another very exciting school year.

Sincerely,
Mark Horowitz
Voice mail: 212-3223
Email: horowimj@milwaukee.k12.wi.us

Please fill out the attached page and return it to Mr. Becker by Thursday if you would like your child to be considered for participation in the Denmark program next year. You can email him at beckerj1@milwaukee.k12.wi.us or call him at 22-3206. There may be more applicants than spaces available, so applying will not guarantee placement in this class.

There will be a Denmark trip meeting for next year's trip on the first Wednesday in June. A $100 deposit will be collected at this meeting. Please make checks payable to Golda Meir School.

APPENDIX

REFLECTION QUESTIONS FOR 15 DAYS

Directions for Pre-Service Teachers: Choose any five of the following reflection questions to answer after reading 15 days.

1. Choose a wow and a wonder based on the book (In other words begin your reflection by completing two sentence starters: "I wonder.........." And " Wow, I.....")
2. If you could interview Mr. Horowitz, what questions would you ask him and why?
3. Reflect on your own elementary school years and your social studies education; compare and contrast your experiences to those of Room 23.
4. What will you take away from this book in regards to your future teaching career?
5. If you could interview any of the children who have participated in this program, what five questions would

you ask them and why?

6. If you were to replicate this experience for your future students, what destination would you choose and why? Design a skeletal outline of your trip(what would you do, where would you go, etc...)
7. Is fourth grade too young to travel internationally? Defend your response.
8. Using visual images, make a drawing (or create a piece of art) that explains your impressions of 15 Days.
9. Are teachers like Mark Horowitz a rare breed? Explain your response.
10. Using the 5 component areas of Social studies, create a lesson plan related to the Denmark experience that could be taught, before, during and after the Denmark trip. Choose 1 of the 5 areas for your lesson.
11. What reflections do you have that have not been addressed by any of the above listed questions or statements?

APPENDIX C

REMEMBERING DENMARK-A REFLECTION
BY A PARENT CHAPERONE, JANET LEW CARR

As every fairytale begins,
"Once upon a time, when magic and dreams were real
A Golda Meir class conjured up a cultural exchange with the Danes.
For 2 weeks, they lived as the Danes and explored the mysteries of Denmark.

Captured in photo journals are impressions of
Copper tops and cobbled walks,
Bigger-than-life sculptures and monuments,
Castles, casements and enchanted forests,
Cemeteries and gnarled ancient trees,
Canals and swans,
Viking myths, ships, runes and relics,
Enshrined royal spirits and crowned jewels,

The glow of candlelight with meals and goodwill,
Copenhagen, Odense, Elsinore, Hillerod, Roskilde, and more,
Laughing children,
Teary children,
Curious(sometimes mischievous) children,
Contended children.

More than the kilograms of souvenirs carried home,
More than the kilometers on foot,bike,train,ferry, car and plane traveled,
They remember the 'hygge' of the Danes, 'the warmth and ooziness,'
The generosity,hospitality and their new friends."

And, the bonuses:
Pulling together as a community, we all made a dream come true.
As one of five parents on our trip,
I was proud to chaperone 20%, James, Kristy, Steven, Keisha and Adam!

APPENDIX

PROCLAMATION

Mayor John Norquist
Milwaukee City Hall
200 East Wells
Milwaukee, Wisconsin 53202

Dear Mayor Norquist:

On behalf of Mr. Mark Horowitz grade class at Golda Meir School, I am writing to request a "Mayor's Proclamation" extending peace and friendship to the people of Gentofte from the people of Milwaukee.

Our dream of visiting Denmark is becoming a reality as we collect passports and plan details for our trip, March 1-15, 1995. Since September 1994, our class of

28 students and their families have weighed possibilities, fundraised for airfare, studied the Danish language and culture, corresponded with host families at Dyssegardsskolen, and developed a special sense of community. Above all, our children are preparing for an experience to be long remembered.

Our children will be living in Hellerup, just outside of Copenhagen. Hellerup is a section of Gentofte which is similar to a county here. If you would like to address your proclamation to the mayor of Gentofte, his name is Hans Toft.

Our children will be attending school with their hosts at Dyssegardsskolen. In translation, "dysse" refers to an ancient burial ground. "Gard" is a farmhouse, and "kolen" is a school. Apparently, many of the schools in Gentofte were built on sites of old farms. Also, the host families are welcoming us into their homes, requesting no stipends. We will explore Gentofte and Copenhagen, and hopefully absorb a deeper understanding of a world culture as well as who we are as Americans.

It would be a privilege to deliver your proclamation to Denmark. We plan to journal our experiences, and would enjoy sharing them with you. If you have any questions, please contact Janet Lew Carr at XXX-XXXX. Thank you for your attention.

Sincerely,
Mr. M. Horowitz's 4th Grade Class
Golda Meir School

APPENDIX 

Discipline Policy

Mark Horowitz Room 23 Golda Meir School

We have a limited number of rules in our classroom. They basically are:

- Each student is expected to work hard. They are expected to complete all work on time. This includes classroom assignments as well as homework assignments.
- Each student is expected to behave well in class. This entails listening attentively when someone is talking to them, following directions carefully, and working quietly when this is appropriate. They are also expected to behave well around the school, including in the hallways, in specialists' rooms, in the lunchroom, and on the playground.
- Each student is expected to treat other students with respect. They do not make comments that would hurt

another child's feelings. They do not take actions that would have the same effect.

If the rules are broken, we would take one or more of the following actions:

- Discuss the misbehavior with the child who has broken the rules. This is done individually, usually during recess or the lunch hour.
- Have the child write down what they did, why it was wrong, and what they plan to do in the future.
- Have the child write a letter to their parents explaining what they did. These notes must be brought back the next school day signed by a parent.
- Call the parent to discuss the problem.
- Have the child work under the supervision of another teacher until they are ready to resume working with our class.
- Have the parent come to school to meet with us and the child.

REFERENCES

Email /Facebook Interviews with:

Mrs. Miriam Meisler
Mrs. Cynthia Weeks
Ms. Heather Felton
Mrs. Jean Gatz
Mrs. Doreen Timmermann
Charlotte, Torben, Victor and William

Hansel, Bettina (1984). *Literature Review: Studies of the Impact of a Travel-Abroad Experience.* (retrieved at: www.bettinahansel.com)

Palmer, Michael (2003). *Student travel offers many educational benefits.* SchooltoursofAmerica.com.

www.helium.com. Educational travel and the benefits to children.

Contributing authors:

Tamara Mcgee Andersen
Karen Banes
Tricia Lye
Sharon Meyer
Mark Schenker
Linda Shortell

Personal Interviews with:

Mrs. Susan Odegard
Ms. Janet Carr
Ms. Suzanne Aschoff
Ms. Heather Aschoff
Mr. Adam Carr
Mrs. Eddneata Thompson
Mr. Mark Horowitz
Mr. Dick Marx
Mr. Tom Hanley
Ms. Ellen Crozier
Mr. Albin Kazmarek

Phone Interviews with:

Mr. Scott Middlestadt
Dr. Mary Horowitz
Ms. Susan Horowitz
Dr. Miriam Meisler
Mrs. Dawn Nystrom

Survey Confirms Travel Abroad at a Young Age Enhances Education, Career Growth and Success. (2011). Obtained from www.wystc.org

Thernstrom, Abigail & Thernstrom, Stephan (2003). *No Excuses: Closing the Racial Gap In Learning.* Simon & Schuster Paperbacks, New York, New York.

Made in the USA
Monee, IL
26 October 2022

16590636R00075